C000126929

DATING
with a FULL DECK

Joe & Julie
Thank you
Much Love.

Kevin M
11/29/2022
610 212-9878

KEVIN MCLEMORE

Dating With A Full Deck, copyright © 2022, by P. Kevin McLemore
Cover, card, and interior design by www.formatting4U.com

All rights reserved. No part of this book may be reproduced in any form or by any electronic or mechanical means, including information storage and retrieval systems—except in the case of brief quotations embodied in critical articles or reviews—without permission in writing from the author.

"In *Dating With A Full Deck*, Kevin shares his personal stories about love, life, romance and dating. This book is a great read for any person in any stage of their dating journey - married for several years or newly single and starting to date. Kevin is a gifted storyteller, and you will find yourself engrossed in his life's stories and the pieces of wisdom and advice he offers."

Lily Siravo
Vice President
The Higgins Group, Inc.

ACKNOWLEDGMENTS

This may come as a surprise to Lisa McLemore (my ex-wife and the mother of three of my four children), but this book would not exist without her. I will forever be indebted to her for the lessons our relationship taught me. From the beginning, we were mismatched. It was only after our divorce that I realized that our incompatibilities were something we could've discovered early on had we only dated differently.

I know it was difficult for her to live with a dreamer like me, and it was unfair of me to expect her to live with uncertainty when doing so has always made her feel unsafe. Even if we weren't suited for each other, we each emerged from our marriage with innumerable blessings. We raised three incredible children and it was our ending that made our new beginnings possible.

I've learned a lot from all my romantic relationships, but my marriage to Lisa offered invaluable insights for which I will never stop being grateful.

As human beings, we are wired for relationships. The relationships that have meant the most to me are the ones I have with my children: Lakisha, Alexander, Theodore, and Jillian. They have given me a greater purpose in life and being their father has taught me how to love.

I would also like to thank my friends Jodi O'Neal, Karen Fraley, Les Brown, Gladys Knight, Karl and Stevie Eller, Sukhy Javeed, Jacquelyn Robinson, and countless others. Their belief and encouragement were essential to the realization of this dream.

Thank you to my late grandparents, Joseph and Annie Phillips, whose successful long-term marriage helped shape my understanding of relationships. Thank you to Bill Daniels, "Uncle Bill," for teaching me to practice integrity and to honor my word; to my cousins, Ron and Betty Green, for teaching me the value of hard work; and to all the other members of my family: Daria Dillard, Dwight Dillard, Dwayne Dillard, Yolanda Dillard, Leroy McLemore Jr., Tammara McLemore, Tonya Dillard, the late Ronda Peters, Raymond N. McLemore, Anthony Daniels, Brandy McLemore, the late James Anthony Daniels, and Theresa Kelly. I am grateful that, despite occasional differences, we have always laughed more than we've cried.

I owe a special debt of gratitude to my coaching clients for sharing the ups and downs of their love lives and trusting me to support them in developing healthy relationships, not just healthy bodies. A special shout-out to Richard LaGravenese, one of my former personal training clients. Richard told me I was the worst writer he had ever met, but I could tell a story like no other, which has enabled me to publish three books before this and make a movie about my book, *The Indispensable Game of X's and O's, How I Learned Everything I'd Ever Need To Know About Life by Playing High School Football.*

Thank you to Daralyse Lyons, my editor, whose relentless pursuit to bring out the very best in me is reflected in these pages.

I also wanted to give thanks to my first editor Sileta Hodge, whose wisdom kept me from tossing my now award-winning book, *Sprinkles, The True Spirit of Christmas,* into the trash. I don't know where I would be without your vision of what I could be as a writer. Due to health reasons, we could not finish this book together, but keep this in mind: you are part of this team and there will be another project, just get better.

Judi Fennell, the voice of Sprinkles, makes the audio book unforgettable and timeless. Thank you for your performance. I am over the top with appreciation for all you do and have done for me as both a friend and author. As I talk about in *Bring in the Closer*, you are the one "just getting it done" right, and on time. You are the best. Thank you for bringing *Dating With A Full Deck* down the home stretch.

There are many, many more I could list. Over the course of my life, I have been uplifted by a lot of people and screwed over by others. All of it has shaped my character and my perspectives.

I think it is only fitting that I began by thanking my first wife because, without understanding my short comings and the parts I played in the demise of that relationship, there would be lots of words on these pages that would not be the words of my own truth, growth, and deeper understanding of human behavior.

Monika Hill, you are my kryptonite. For better or worse, Monika is someone who always strives to be the best version of herself. When we first met, I realized we brought out the best in each other. I will forever appreciate her insights, feedback, support, and encouragement. She believes in my dreams and enables me to do the same. She is my light in the darkness, and, while neither of us is perfect and our relationship isn't either, we both like *and* love each other. I am convinced that our love is as strong as it is because we came to dating with a full deck, raw and totally vulnerable. Just like peeling back the skin of a banana to reach the fruit, so it is with human behavior; you must peel back all the outer layers to see your own truth. So, with that said, thank you for being the calm in my storm.

I DEDICATE THIS BOOK TO

My parents, Leroy McLemore Sr., and Norma Jean Lartigue, and to my children, Lakisha, Alexander, Theodore, and Jillian, plus Connor. My parents brought me into the world, and, in my darkest days, it was my love for my children that offered me a reason to live and a pathway to love and kindness toward others. Always "Reach One, Teach One."

TABLE OF CONTENTS

FOREWORD

Dating With A Full Deck is a brilliant and profound perspective which greatly values both men and women. Connecting and helping others as a dating educator and professional photographer is like the nature of Kevin's career as a Fitness professional, award-winning author, paid speaker, and lifestyle coach. We both have witnessed fit, talented, and intelligent clients who have suffered through hardships and end up forgetting their inner beauty. We live in a fast-paced, superficial society where most focus on the wrong things, constantly finding fault within themselves. Kevin's book helps you find and accept yourself *first,* while challenging you to get clear about what you want. Kevin also encourages you to articulate and ask for what you're looking for because we deserve it. Most importantly, we are good enough just the way we are.

The online dating culture is a hot-or-not game geared around many stereotypes. *Dating With A Full Deck* has the secret ingredient for being successful in the modern dating world. It truly serves as a dating coach, wingman, wing woman, and best friend. Kevin writes directly to the heart of single women, reminding us that we have more power than we think— that *we* hold the cards. But, if we don't come from an authentic and truthful place, a pretty face and winning smile will only go so far. A common mistake women make is hiding our imperfections that men fall in love with. In doing so, we lose the opportunity to show who we are as a person while creating a house of cards with no foundation.

What I love about this book is Kevin's ability to tell a story like no other. He draws from his life of working with others and his understanding of interpersonal relationship skills. He took the knowledge he gained while dealing with people's personal needs from various backgrounds and created this helpful, creative, and easily consumable content.

1

Kevin loves nothing more than helping others and setting people up for success, while also encouraging those struggling in the confusing world of online dating. Life is a great educator, and the best lessons and learning experience come from the school of hard knocks. Lucky for all of us—readers as well as singles—you can improve your dating skills dramatically with each chapter.

Dating With A Full Deck is *your* next chapter—an opportunity for brand new opportunities and possibilities. After reading this book, you'll have takeaways that better prepare you for your next big date or new relationship. This book encourages you to look for someone with whom you share common interests and, most importantly, to be yourself. Unfortunately, most people come at dating all wrong. People spend all their time trying to be an unrealistic version of themselves when the secret is putting yourself out there while being vulnerable and showing your real authentic self.

This book and deck of fifty-four cards which are part of the book, provide strategies and tools that, if applied on dates, will have truthful and fun conversations that will have you quickly understanding if this person is right for you. It takes all the pressure away around saying the wrong thing, anxiety around these first encounters, and the general fear of dating. Pain and experience have been Kevin's greatest teacher, and this book is a wealth of information, which embodies his insight and wisdom around relationships and dating. This book is a must-read for anyone starting over or new to online dating.

Kerry Brett
Author and The Podcast Host of Shot@love

INTRODUCTION

When my first marriage came to a screeching halt, I was forced to confront the fact that I had no idea how to be single. After more than twenty-two years with one person, I had to rediscover who I was in a dating context. What made this task even more daunting was that, when Lisa and I met, there'd been no such thing as online dating or "Netflix and chill."

It was 2013, I found myself released into the dating wild, and, after several months of trying to navigate the "rules" of dating in a modern world, I decided I didn't want to date like everybody else. I wanted to date like myself.

Luckily, in dealing with people from all walks of life as a professional lifestyle and fitness coach, I had already come to learn a lot about the ways people strive for what they want and the ways they sabotage themselves. That didn't prevent me from falling flat on my face as I attempted to navigate the world of dating post-divorce, but it did equip me to embark on a different kind of dating and to emerge from that process not only with love in my life but with the invaluable lessons that I offer in this book.

Love is a basic human need. Without it, we can't survive. So, if everyone needs and wants love, why is it so hard to get it, find it, and keep it?

I have come to believe that people struggle to find lasting love because they don't know how to be transparent and authentic. They go into dating looking to find a "great catch," but when did finding a potential soulmate become akin to casting a line and getting someone "on the hook"?

My intention for *Dating With A Full Deck* is not to provide a how-to book for getting into a long-term relationship or marriage, nor is it to offer a quick swipe-right hook-up book—which will leave you feeling satisfied for a night, but empty shortly after.

This book provides a tangible set of tools that, if applied to your interactions, will lead to the kinds of truthful conversations that will allow you to figure out whether or not you've met someone compatible. You don't have to try to figure out the "rules" of dating or play games that will leave you depleted and confused. Instead, reading this book will help you to create an environment that will allow you to truly have open and honest conversations with someone you're romantically interested in, something that has become ever more difficult in modern-day society. And, although there are no conventional dating games in this book, it is accompanied by a fun and informative deck of fifty-two cards (plus a couple of jokers). Bring this deck with you on your first handful of dates with someone new. They can act as a helpful conversation starter and will have you laughing together and learning about each other. I've even given the questions on the cards to couples who have been together for a while and, without exception, they've reported that the questions deepened their connection.

My goal for *Dating With A Full Deck* is to allow fun and free-flowing dialogue.

We live in an image-driven, instant-gratification world, especially in the online dating space where we attract potential partners physically first and expect emotions to develop later. In today's dating world, cell phone apps have replaced chance meetings, meet-ups, and introductions from family and friends. This means that if you make it to a first date with someone, you're almost guaranteed to have a physical attraction (provided someone doesn't put misleading photos on their profile), and it also means that mental and emotional attraction isn't a foregone conclusion.

Dating might begin superficially, but successful relationships are far more substantial. *Dating With A Full Deck* will help you determine your capacity to connect with someone in the long term. And having a predetermined set of topics to talk about can make meeting a new person a whole lot less awkward.

I had a personal training client who used to complain about never making it past the first date, and, after several months of training together, I finally realized his problem. He didn't know what to talk about or how to relate. He's an incredible guy and once he gets to know someone, he can be a great conversationalist, but he is shy and a bit socially awkward. He'd do well via texting or on an app because he had time to think about his replies, but face-to-face, across the table from a stranger, he was at a loss for words. I started giving him a list of topics to talk about and he started getting second and third and fourth dates. Pretty soon, he was the one deciding whether he was interested and not the other way around. I came up with the question idea because of my personal experiences.

When I re-entered the dating arena, I started paying close attention to people, both young and old, who were out on dates, trying to get dates or talking about how much they hated dating. I quickly realized that even seasoned daters knew about as much as I did about new age courtship (not a lot), and that the way most people date puts a lot of pressure onto them and their potential partners.

I'd been interested in dating and relationships even before I found myself newly single after twenty-two years as a married man. I even referred to myself as "the original Hitch" because of how much I loved setting people up. I can still vividly recall fixing one of my female training clients up with a good friend (who I will refer to as Matt because he's now happily married with children, and I'd rather not have his wife kick my butt for trying to act as his self-appointed matchmaker before he met and married her). My training client had been telling me for the better part of the year that she wanted to meet a "good guy." I knew a great guy! The aforementioned "Matt" had been a friend of mine for years and had been telling me he was looking for a young lady with whom he could share his life. Matt was a kind and generous person—the exact person my training client had described. So, I hooked them up.

He picked her up at her door with flowers—an old school move—in a chauffeured car, took her to one of the three five-star restaurants he owned, and, when it was over, walked her to her building door and asked to see her again. She promised to call, took his number, and never called.

When I saw her for her next training session, she told me she did not want to see Matt again because he was too nice of a guy and she was afraid she would hurt him. My response was "WTF? After one date you are afraid you'd hurt him? Haven't you been telling me you *want* a nice guy?"

After listening to her retell the events of their date, I realized that although she was initially impressed by him, she felt as if the date had lacked chemistry and was hurt that he hadn't put the moves on her. Poor

V

Matt never knew that she had put on her very best sexy underwear, shaved her legs, and sweetened her breath, just in case. Once I spoke to my client, I understood the problem: neither she nor Matt had made their desires clear and, as a result, they never got past the first date.

When I began going on my dates, I started to see just how often people weren't being upfront about what they wanted and expected from each other. But they also weren't asking the questions that would lead them to open up to one another. I started asking.

Dating With A Full Deck is not a guaranteed pathway to marriage, nor is it a player's manual for a quick hook-up. It will help you to be more self-revealing and to invite others to be open and honest with you. Whether or not your first date with that next someone is your last first date ever because you meet your life partner or whether you buy this book and spend several months or years in your search for lasting love, this book was created to provide you with better dating experiences and redirect the social dating behavior. Some of this may change your life or create a better perspective and interpretation of what you think you understand about a first date. Meeting "the one" is great. The quality of our lives is determined by the quality of our relationships. But whether you meet "the one" today, tomorrow or a year from now, it's essential you acquire the skills to let others see the true you because that's what it takes to fall and stay in love.

CHAPTER ONE

How Does Dating With A Full Deck *Work?*

It's Friday night, you're out at the bar. Across the room, you spot a sexy stranger. You feel the connection between the two of you. Something compels you to approach and introduce yourself. When you do, you strike up an immediate and easy conversation. You arrange a date. Within a few weeks, you've entered a relationship. Sound like a familiar scenario? Not likely. These days, in the world of swiping left and right, it's difficult navigating the world as a single person.

You might stumble upon someone whose outward appearance draws you in, or whose personality you think is wonderful, but it can feel impossible to take that long walk across the room to approach a total stranger or to take the mental and emotional leap of telling a platonic friend you're interested in more.

Consider *Dating With A Full Deck* as your own personal wingman, woman, or person. In this book, I'll provide you with a useful set of tools you can use to enter a meaningful dialogue with someone you know or someone you don't.

This book has nothing to do with any standard card game, but it comes with a deck of fifty-four cards that will make dating fun, engaging, and honest. Each card contains a question which, after you shuffle the deck and pull a card at random, you present that question to the person you're with (or the one you want to be with).

Early dating should be about having a good time while getting to know someone and having them get to know you. By allowing you to talk openly about what you're willing or not willing to do, what subjects or topics you are open to talking about, and those you'd rather not discuss,

Dating With A Full Deck eliminates awkward silences, boredom, and even unintentional overshares.

There is no such thing as a perfect person or a perfect date yet being open from the outset will set you up to discover whether or not you have found someone who brings out the best in you and vice versa. Each chapter provides various insights about dating, love, and the early stages of a new relationship, and each card acts as a conversation springboard.

The book works especially well if both parties have read it prior to a first date, but that's not necessary. As long as one party has read the book and looked at the accompanying cards, you'll have all the ingredients for a great first date. Who knows? Start *Dating With A Full Deck* and your next first date just might end up being your last first date.

I remember the day of my first date. It was our big family trip for the summer at Kings Island, an amusement park in Mason, Ohio. It started out blazing hot. I was dressed in shorts and what is now called a muscle shirt (a tight t-shirt). It was midafternoon when, suddenly, the sky opened. We were near the Ferris wheel and the area was packed. My brother and I sought shelter under one of the game canopies. I had a towel with me to dry the sweat off my body. Out of nowhere, this beautiful mocha queen dashed under the canopy right next to me, soaked. My heart skipped a beat. I'm not sure if I had any game about me then, but without asking permission and without a formal introduction, I took my unused towel and placed it over her shoulders to dry her off. I didn't give any thought as to what could happen if she took offense at my random act of kindness and kicked me in the balls. I placed my towel over her shoulder, not knowing if I was risking my life or would get arrested for touching a stranger. My intentions were good. It turned out to be one of the best days of my life, my first kiss and relationship that would last for years and see the birth of my first child eight years later. This was truly dating with a full deck raw.

CHAPTER TWO

Men Are Simple: "SIMPLY WHEN"

When I polled my single male friends about what they were looking for in a woman, without fail, every one of them told me they wanted someone good-looking, smart, and fit, who was also hardworking, motivated, independent, devoted, an excellent cook, loved to laugh, and could get along with their friends. That seemed like a tall order. No wonder they were single!

I thought back to what my married friends had claimed to want back when they'd been single and realized that they'd wanted the exact same things. When I was single, I'd have said I wanted those same things, too. When I was married, I'd have said I wanted them too. And yet, while my first marriage had been phenomenal on paper, it hadn't possessed the necessary synchronicity of values and personalities required for a marriage that would require death to part us. My second marriage was less about two people trying to be perfect on their own and create something perfect together, and more about growing together as two imperfect and like-minded people.

If you take a good look around and observe successful couples, you won't see many men with women who are brilliant, have rock-hard bodies, scored in the top ninety-five percent on their SATs, and love watching sports with them on Sundays. And you will not see many women with men who check all their boxes either. Men tend to gravitate toward women who are independent, hard to catch, kind, and make them feel important. This isn't an accident. Underneath all their purported machismo, most men are looking for a mate who will protect their hearts and do and say things that support his vision of himself as indispensable to her. Men aren't complicated. If a man feels like a

3

woman is in his corner and has his back, he's attracted to her, and, if the timing is right, he'll be invested from the outset.

In our society, we are socially conditioned to believe that men are tough, but the reality is that there are more Fat Alberts in the world than Magic Mikes. And though we know this, most of us want a partner who will allow us to be ourselves and not set unrealistic expectations, while simultaneously making us feel special.

It's no secret that many of us hold others—and ourselves—to higher standards than might be obtainable. We want to look like professional models or athletes, have millions in the bank, and keep up with the Joneses (and the Smiths and the Roberts and everyone we see on Instagram). This isn't to say that human beings shouldn't continue to evolve, but only that perfection is an unrealistic and unhealthy standard. Although we may be successful on several levels at any given time, there will also be other levels where we're failing.

Let's say a man graduated with honors and received a master's degree from one of the best schools in the country, then went on to get a job for one of the biggest and best financial institutions in the world. I know such a man. He has a beautiful home, a lovely wife, and three children. Unfortunately, to keep up with the demands of work, he copes by eating to excess and drinking too much, and, since he has very little time for his wife, his marriage is straining at the seams.

I know another guy who is a dutiful and committed husband and father but doesn't have a college diploma and lives paycheck to paycheck.

I'm not suggesting that there aren't well-rounded people out there or that the price of success in business is relationship failure. I *am* saying that nearly every person who is successful on one level is failing on another. We're all human and none of us can do everything perfectly. No man is invincible, but men have been culturally conditioned to strive to attain whatever set of standards his partner sets for him/partner. If he can't, he'll resent her and feel ashamed of himself. No matter where a guy is in his life or whatever level he is now playing on, a man is looking for a partner who will stand *beside* him, not *on* him. We are in a time where words matter, although the words on the next pages of this book, may seem to be more directed in a heterosexual relationship, my social circle is inclusive. The conversation beyond this paragraph should be understood as that I am talking about and speaking to partners. Human behavior when attached to relationships is inclusive of your personal choice of your partner's gender.

I want to share the story of Frank and Susan. These are fake names for the sake of anonymity. Frank was a real go-getter, hard worker, win-at-all costs kind of guy. Frank met Susan during the process of going through a horrible divorce from his first wife. A devoted father, his failed marriage drove him deeper into work mode and left little time for any matters of the heart. This was his mindset until a visit to the dentist's office changed it. When Frank entered the waiting room, the only seat available—which he took—was near an average, but an attractive woman. The two greeted each other. There was a dramatic pause between hellos. Before either one knew it, the conversation seemed to just flow.

Susan was a few years younger than Frank, friendly, and totally different from his soon-to-be ex-wife. His ex was all about money and keeping up with the Joneses. She was the opposite of Frank, who was more of a living-in-the-moment kind of guy. Susan and Frank hit it off well. Susan was a little more aggressive and freer-spirited. She was a try-anything kind of girl, something Frank was not used to. But the two got along and their conversations seem to always flow smoothly, making it easy for Frank to be emotionally open with her.

It took a couple of years before Frank would go all-in with Susan. But there was not a day that they did not talk or see each other. Susan made space in a couple of drawers for Frank's things. Over time, little by little, each empty drawer somehow got filled until the day Frank got a key to the house and a bay for his car. It was a relationship three years in the making and a perfect fit for both.

Frank was determined that the next woman he allowed into his heart would have to be emotionally invested and supportive of his dreams. Frank had always wanted to have a business of his own that would free him from the grind of chasing someone else's dream. And, as life would have it, as soon as things were going well for Frank and Susan, it all turned to crap when Frank fell and broke his neck at work. Frank endured two years of hell, going for surgery after surgery to be free of the never-ending pain.

Susan, from the outside, seemed to be one hundred percent in support of Frank. She was an all-or-nothing kind of woman, of which Frank was unaware. Frank thought he had little to worry about regarding his relationship with Susan. Unfortunately, Susan's try-anything-once attitude attracted another. This created a dramatic rift in their relationship when Frank discovered her selfish needs. As painful as it was for Frank, every hardship has a silver lining. Frank turned his heart back to his faith. Susan did the same and grew up. To this day, they are still together.

For most of us looking in, we would have suggested Frank move on. We must understand that our own happiness is predicated on the needs of each of us as individuals and not the recommendations of those sitting on the sidelines. We like to think that all men are out to run the bases at a world record pace. For some men, this is true, as well as for some more progressive women. But when it comes to his needs and her needs, men are simple, women are complicated, and in the case of Frank and Susan, they are both playing this game with a full deck.

Chapter Three

What A Woman Wants… "The Never-Ending Story"

I can still vividly recall sitting in my mother's kitchen when she told my sisters, "Do not give up that one thing until you make your man walk over hell and through high waters. He has to earn it."

I am not the first to break the "man code" by telling the women reading this that they are entitled to respect and men are never entitled to sex. When it comes to romance, women hold all the cards (no pun intended). I have daughters, and I have let each of them know that it is their right and their responsibility to dictate the pace for physical intimacy. Unfortunately, the emphasis on "waiting" can sometimes make it seem as if all men are sex-crazed perverts and all women are prudes.

As I embarked on this book-writing project, I interviewed more than a hundred men and women, and what I learned from the women I spoke to was incredibly illuminating. Almost without exception, women told me that one of their deepest needs was the need for affection—not merely emotional affection, but physical as well. Attention and affection are essential for women—and this does not necessarily mean sex. Any man who wants a quality relationship would do well to learn that sex exists on a spectrum and that, for most women, there is more to connection than penetration.

If you are a woman reading this book, keep in mind that most men aren't as emotionally bonded as you are in the beginning. They do not understand that sex for you is the physical expression of an emotional bond. If you are a man reading this, realize that offering a woman your undivided attention and taking the time to get to know her essence, and not just try to get into her pants, is an important part of the seduction dance.

While putting this book together, I came up with a hundred and eighty questions and then sent those questions to twenty separate couples to ask them to help me narrow it down to fifty-four (54 cards, plus two jokers). I asked each partner to highlight his or her selections—men's picks in blue and women's in pink. To my surprise, every woman highlighted all the questions that had to do with sex. The men, on the other hand, had only one question when it came to sex: in a relationship, do you use sex as a weapon?

The point I want to make in this chapter is that women have a lot of power when it comes to sex and intimacy, and they also have a lot of desires that can sometimes go unrecognized. Sex for a man is the relationship equivalent of air and water. He needs it. Sex for a woman is often more complicated, but if we expand our concept of sex to include intimacy in general, the chances are that men and women both have essential needs that cannot remain unmet without catastrophic consequences.

The more truthful you are with yourself and your potential partner about your needs, the easier it will be for them to meet those needs. I am not suggesting talking about sex on a first or even a second date. I am suggesting talking about sex before you have it. You will want to know, prior to becoming physically intimate, the way the person you're interested in views sex, monogamy, intimacy, and relationships in general.

If a relationship becomes physical too quickly, there will not be enough time to connect on an emotional level and know whether you're a match. I remember working with a female client once who had a phrase that always stuck with me: sex goggles. She claimed that, once she had sex with a man, she could no longer see him accurately, which, I told her, was even more reason to wait. Men must be invested first to appreciate the person they are with. Women must see a man clearly before deciding whether or not to give him the gift of herself. Having said that, do not get it twisted. When it comes to sex, men and women are both equally capable of feeling desire; they just may experience it differently.

I am going to share a story about the only one-night stand I ever had and what I didn't know at that time. About a hundred years ago, the much younger and single Kevin was so focused on becoming a world-class athlete that there was little to no time for any kind of relationship. However, the one thing I longed for was the fairytale romance that seemed to only exist on the pages of a Harlequin romance book (which I have never read, but have been on a couple covers). Yes, I said it! I always have been and always will be a hopeless romantic. Back to the story.

I was in Ohio at this fancy health club called Scandinavian Health Club. This club was the first of its kind back in the day. It was much like Lifetime Fitness and Equinox are today. As I exited from the men's locker room onto the fitness floor, a young lady crossed my path on her way to an aerobics class. She was dressed in Reeboks, tights, and legwarmers (now I am dating myself). Hundreds of incredibly attractive men and women were members of this club, but one thing that stuck out about her was, in the upper right corner of her head, her dark black hair was blessed with a premature steak of grey or white hair. It caught my attention, and kept my attention long after she had passed. For some reason, the inner stalker within me appeared. My attention was diverted from my workout. I had to get a second/better look at this person. So, I followed her to the class. I stood outside the door, waiting to see if she would look up and notice that the guy she had passed on the stairs had followed her. But, like that little boy with a crush on his third-grade teacher, Mary never looked my way.

Remember, I said I was a hopeless romantic. While trying to figure out a way to get her attention, I ran out of the club, hopped into my little MG, and drove to the nearest florist. It was about a mile and a half away from our club. I ordered one dozen red roses and had them delivered to the club with the instructions to give these roses to the only girl in that class who had hair coloring like a skunk. I know it doesn't sound like I had my act together, but I didn't know her name yet and it cost me an extra hundred dollars to have the flowers delivered before the class ended. So, when I was asked what I wanted the card to say, I told the florist to just say that my name was Kevin and I thought she had a beautiful smile. Nothing more.

The roses got to the club faster than I did. I had to stop for gas. Then I had to push my car downhill to pop the clutch because my MG was notorious for starting on its own terms. By the time I got back to the club, the class had ended. But Mary was standing in the class holding a dozen red roses. The delivery person had interrupted the aerobics class yelling, "Is there anyone here with a grey streak in their hair like a skunk?" Lucky for me, Mary was the only one. Not thinking this through, I saw Mary with the flowers and about a dozen or so women from the class around her. She was trying to figure out who sent the flowers to her and failed to sign their name on the card. Well, it did not take long for Mary to figure out who sent the flowers because shortly after she walked out of the class, our paths crossed again.

"Nice flowers," I said. She replied that they'd magically just shown up during the class. Without reservation, her smile stole my heart. I replied, "You have a nice smile." It did not take her long to figure out I was the mystery Rose Guy. We became good friends. For a month or two, there was not much flirting, just casual conversation in passing at the club. One Friday, as the club closed, I was taking the top off the MG. Mary walked over to the car and expressed her interest in it. We talked for about an hour. I took her out in the MG and allowed her to drive back to the club. The MG started without having to push it downhill. Everything was perfect. Mary invited me to her house, and, before I knew it, Friday had turned into Saturday, Saturday into Sunday, and Sunday turned into Sunday night. Monday came the same way as every other day in the week, and I went to work. I called Mary and got her answering machine. Tuesday, Wednesday, Thursday, Friday, and for the next two months, the days and the unanswered calls seem to blend.

One day, our paths crossed in a supermarket. I wasn't sure if our weekend together had been as good for her as it'd been for me. Because I never had a history of casual relationships, I thought, emotionally, we had connected. However, Mary had been emotionally on a whole other level than I'd been. I'd been totally taken by the girl with the grey streak in her hair. Now, face-to-face in the store, I said hello and she replied. I told her she looked great. Mary smiled at me. My heart had been beating over time. Trying to maintain my dignity and cool, I complimented her. It was impossible for Mary to look bad. She was perfect. "Well," she said, "I have to get going. Nice to see you."

What? I'd thought to myself. *This is all she has to say to me after a weekend that played out more like a scene from Pretty Woman?* She turned her cart around, looked at me, paused as if she had something she wanted to say, then headed down the aisle. "Mary," I said. "Did I do something wrong?" "No," she replied. "Why?" "I don't know. We had such a great time that weekend, but, after that, nothing, no calls, voice messages, nothing until now. I was just wondering if there was something I did to turn you off." Mary walked back over to me and gently put her lips to mine. It was just a peck, not what I was expecting, and neither was what she said next. "You are the all-time best. A gentleman above all gentlemen, a romantic. I could not have dreamed of a more perfect weekend." She kissed me again and this time it was a real kiss. When she pulled away, I smiled, and she smiled back.

I asked if she would like to see me again. She said, "We'll see."

I could not take "We'll see" after two months of not returning my calls. I said, "Mary, we'll *see*?"

Not ever seeing this coming, she called me by my last name and confidently said, "It was just sex. You had a nice ass. It was just sex."

She left me standing there and I never heard from her again. I was crushed, this was a dude's move. Until now, I thought only men played this game. To this day, I still feel used.

My takeaway here is that, if I had known it was just sex going in, I would not have left so many romantic messages on her answering machine.

Chapter Four

Become Your Own Mr./Mrs. Right

The truth is that most of us lack the skills or awareness to address and meet each other's needs. This is not a bad thing. Too many people come to a relationship from a place of scarcity, looking to take from another person what they feel is missing in themselves. This is completely backward. Think about your closest friends. I would imagine that, when it comes to friendships, you look for people with whom you share common interests and can be yourself. I would bet that you don't set out to find friends who are completely without fault or who are exactly like you or are capable of filling in every insufficiency in your life.

When it comes to a successful relationship, it is essential that you recognize that *you're* responsible for meeting your own needs and that it's each partner's role to meet the other's *wants*. That is not to say each person shouldn't have deal-breakers and things that matter to them and requirements they communicate to their partner. However, the more equipped you are to ensure that you are okay as a person separate and distinct from your partner, the better your relationship will be.

I will admit it: in my first marriage, I was too needy. I expected my wife to fill in whatever voids existed in my life and in myself and, conversely, I thought it was my role to ensure that she was always happy. It is no great surprise that, over time, our marriage devolved.

With my wife Monika, I resolved to be different. I came up with a fun way to be good to ourselves and to each other. A few months into our first year of marriage, I went to the grocery store and bought several oversized bags of jellybeans. When I got home, I announced that I wanted us to play a game. Of course, Monika was intrigued. We each counted out one hundred jellybeans and put them in individual glass vases. Then, we counted another one hundred jellybeans and put them in a vase of their own. There were a lot of leftover jellybeans that we stored in a container in the cabinet. Then I told her to pick a vase for herself, one for me, and one for our relationship.

She wanted to know the purpose of the jellybeans and the vases. I explained that I wanted us to start off from a place of abundance, individually and together, while also leaving room to grow and evolve. Every time we had an experience that felt personally enriching and uplifting, we would add a jellybean, and every time we felt like we had let ourselves down, we'd remove one from the jar. On the other hand, when we felt as if we had done something to damage the relationship, we'd take a bean away, and when we did something to improve it, we'd add one.

We agreed that we would tell each other each time we added to or took away from a jar and talk about what had happened (positive or negative) and that we would continue the experiment for three months then count the jellybeans again.

This was one of the most enriching and illuminating things we could have ever done for our relationship. Talking about the things we had gone through during the day, the moments each of us found meaningful, and the times we hurt ourselves and each other—while making the impetus for these conversations' fun and irreverent—enabled us to take responsibility for ourselves and our marriage. We started to add as many jellybeans as possible to our own vases and—surprise, surprise—the relationship vase began to overflow. After the three months were over, we combined all three vases' worth of beans and realized that our initial three hundred had blossomed into six hundred and sixty-five!

When it comes to relationships, needs should be addressed daily as either Deposits or Withdrawals. At the same time, if we forget that we owe it to our partners to take care of our own emotions, we will start to put far too much pressure on the other person. One of the great paradoxes of dating is that, until we can give ourselves what we are looking for from someone else, we can't be happy individually or together. So, even before you go on that first date, start filling your own jar with jellybeans and look for someone who is prepared to do the same.

My grandmother's mother had great wisdom when it came to matters of the heart, and what to look for and what *not* to look for when it came to dating. Her southern upbringing taught her that real gentlemen opened doors and pulled chairs out for women, and if a woman refused this southern gentleman approach that she was no lady and should be left on the curb, and I should invest my time in someone more worthy of my time. It is no secret that I learn so much from what I do for a living now with years of understanding and dealing with people's personal needs from all kinds of backgrounds, as well as what I have been taught by my grandmother and personal relationships.

Understanding his needs and her needs, your relationship education is predicated on what is taught or caught—meaning, what you have learned from your personal experiences and what you've taken away better prepares you for the next relationship, and, at the same time, the damage you hold on to will put you in the same situation that failed you before.

There is no one who can honestly say they are without faults. I, personally, hate useless conversations and people who are invested only in addressing their own needs, or who create a timeline as to when your needs will become important enough to be a topic of conversation. Depending on your interpretation and perception, most of us spend far too much time and energy making sure we meet the needs of our partners, and unconsciously sacrifice our needs and so much more of ourselves without ever addressing the conversation in our head, knowing this conversation needs addressing.

Very few of us ever wants to listen to where we fall short with regards to our own needs, we are always hopeful that our partners will one day get it.

We can ask ourselves, are we asking too much from our partners? Do we just keep our fingers crossed, that our partner gets it, or live with the fact that our partners will never understand the day when it comes, that you are now sick and tired and looking down into an empty jar of jellybeans?

The conversation about your needs and her needs starts with addressing the truth about them and the responsibilities each of you places on your partners' fulfillment of those needs. You should remember that understanding human emotion is based on perception and interpretation. When communicating your needs with your partner, keep in mind that most of the things we claim we need are superficial and will cause more jellybeans to be removed than added.

For example, is being upset about leaving dishes out when the dishwasher is empty and only two feet away from the sink, worth two to three jellybeans out of your jar or is just keeping your mouth shut and putting those dishes in the dishwasher and moving on worth more?

Your happiness is not the responsibility of your partner, it is yours. You cannot be happy with someone else until you have discovered happiness within yourself.

The key here is to bend and not break, to love the way you want to be loved, and to listen and acknowledge that, when you are adding someone to your life, it is not your partner's responsibility to fill your jar with jellybeans. It is your responsibility to make sure your jar is more than full before you add a jar for his or her needs, and well before you are sharing space. Always add more jellybeans than you take away. Think less, live more.

CHAPTER FIVE

Truth Or Truth

My grandfather, the late Joe Phillips, always talked about how important it was for a man to let his woman know her value to him. I cannot remember being around him and my grandmother without him saying something sweet about the way she looked or her personality or thanking her for the way she took care of things and how she made him feel. Being uninitiated in the world of romance, I did not understand the importance of valuing a partner or the fact that doing so could never be a substitute for poor self-esteem.

To use my grandfather's words, "There's never enough praise you can put upon your woman that will make her happy with herself. Her happiness and truth have to come from her."

As a professional trainer and lifestyle coach, I have witnessed firsthand that, no matter how fit, talented, shapely, and smart my female clients are, most of them find fault with themselves and have an unhealthy relationship with the scale. No matter how fit they are, there is that number they are chasing that seems never to be caught. I blame the media, the fashion industry, the scale in the gym/bathroom, and a society in which being good or special to your mate will never be good enough.

As much as I have tried to convince them to appreciate themselves as they are and for all they have accomplished, most still do not see themselves the way the outside world—especially men—sees them. This is difficult, especially when it comes to dating.

I guarantee you that you have known a woman (perhaps, several women—perhaps, even yourself) who have settled for less in the realm of men. Countless beautiful, kind, considerate, ambitious women are currently wasting their time with deadbeat men. Why? If we do not value ourselves, we don't demand it. What we deserve is the truth.

A pivotal part of dating is to evaluate yourself accurately and honestly, to know your worth and what you can contribute to a relationship. There are countless stories out there of people who lie about their height, weight, and age on online dating profiles. That is just a small example of a larger pattern of deception. People start relationships being dishonest with each other; much of this stems from their inability to be honest with themselves.

I have come to believe from my experience with clients and all my successful and failed relationships that it is essential to compliment the one you are with, to uplift them, and let them know all the wonderful qualities they possess. Keep complimenting them, and not just about the superficial stuff. Yes, tell them they look great, but also tell them you value their intellect, their motivation, and the way they make you feel, and how confident they are about themselves, and that their independence is a turn-on. The better-rounded you are in your discussions and observations, the better your intimacy, in and out of the bedroom.

At the same time, it is essential for you to learn how to internalize positive feedback and how not to get consumed in negative self-assessment. We all have features and qualities that are admirable and others that are not. The more you can acknowledge what you like about yourself, the easier it will be to know your worth when it comes to dating and relationships.

We live in a world where most of us claim to want to find a partner who can reflect what we deem to be a good catch to share our lives, our time, and our wealth. However, despite wanting this very reasonable and attainable thing, we then add a lot of unnecessary pressure onto ourselves, our prospective partners, and the situation. We say we are looking for someone who has ambition, intelligence, fitness, positivity, a soul connection, and everything under the sun, but we never bother to acknowledge that some of the qualities we say we're looking for directly contradict each other.

What use is it to find an ambitious man if he is never home because he must work eighty-hour work weeks to secure enough income to qualify as "ambitious enough"? What use is it to meet and marry the "perfect" woman, when she is perfect on the outside but emasculates her man every time she thinks he is feeling too good about himself?

There are innumerable ways that we strive for things that are not compatible and then end up feeling like, even if we get what we are after, we have lost in the end.

When it comes to inviting someone else into your life, it is important to honestly assess your wants and needs. An honest dialogue enables you to own what you want and what you have to offer. Think about this: if you got an interview for your "dream" job, you would show up with an updated version of your resume and put your best foot forward, but you wouldn't lie about your qualifications or benefit and salary requirements because you'd know that doing so would only get you fired if you managed to secure the position on a lie.

It might sound cliché, but relationships involve work. You want to know going into a new one what the job entails.

Men are conditioned from early on in life to define themselves by their careers and their income, whereas women are told to derive their sense of self from their place in the household, their family, and their homes. If you ask any man who he is, his response will likely be about his job, his position in his job, if he is successful in that job, and/or his ability to provide for himself and his loved ones. If you ask a woman the same question, she is far more likely to talk about her family, her friends, her prospective life partner, and her vision for her life. This is not to say this observation is foolproof, but it is based on my experience, research, and the structures of society.

Both men and women enter relationships with a purpose, and, although those purposes overlap, it is useful to know that there might be differences and that the sooner both sides accept and acknowledge this, the easier it becomes to create something that will make both parties happier together than they ever were alone.

I have learned from the men I've interviewed, worked with, lived alongside, helped to raise, and from being a man myself, that if a man values and respects a woman, no matter his dating history, he will do everything he can to treat her right.

Part of being able to connect with someone else is understanding where they are coming from and listening for what is and isn't being said. If you find yourself sitting across from a man who sees something in you that he has never seen in any other, he will walk on fire barefoot to keep your attention and make you feel special.

The power of the women's liberation movement has done a lot for supporting women's independence, which, in my opinion, has almost all been positive. Equal pay in the workplace should be a foregone conclusion. We need to celebrate our partner's independence, strive for more emotional balance on both sides, increase our sensitivity, and praise balance over striving for perfection.

Today's women are often equally or more successful in the business world than their male counterparts. They are self-supporting, driven, and goal oriented. For most women, having a man in their life is an option rather than a necessity. That means that, for both men and women, it is essential to acknowledge that the most tangible benefits of modern-day relationships between equals are emotional. We are not entering into dating requiring someone to pay the bills, do the housework, or anything else. These days, you do not even need a partner to conceive a child. Although this is wonderful because it enables us to focus on establishing and maintaining a quality connection, it also requires greater transparency and vulnerability.

For men, who have been conditioned to see themselves as "providers," it can challenge their ego to know that they are not necessary. Many men struggle to find a place and a position in a woman's life, let alone her heart. Therefore, it is helpful to tell him all the things you like about him and to believe you when he tells you what he likes about you. If you are a man reading this book, know that there is so much more available to you when you get honest about the fact that you're not indispensable and, therefore, you need to be dependable.

Relationships are not easy. The good ones take work. But they are worth it and once we acknowledge that what we're looking for is someone we can be ourselves with and, at the same time, who we want to be better for, we can come to dating from a place of abundance rather than with a mindset of scarcity.

When you go on your next date, I dare you to be at least ninety-five percent honest with the person sitting across from you. We are all prone to a little first-date embellishment, but if you can bring ninety-five percent of yourself to the (literal) table, you just might find someone who will come to love you exactly as you are.

Spoiler alert: if you make it to a first date, the physical attraction is assuredly already there. All that is left is to see beyond the surface, and you can only do that if you take the risk to dare to be your ninety-five percent unfiltered self.

Dare to be truthful. Open your mind. Let go of the drama and the heartache of past failed relationships. Be crazy in your heart, not in your head. You've no doubt heard of the game "truth or dare." I am going to suggest a game of both. I dare you to be honest.

When I was much younger, my path crossed with a young lady that was J-Lo beautiful. She was so beautiful that I had to convince her that she could do better than the one she was with. Of course, that better meant me. At least, that is what I thought. Seventy-two hours after my indecent proposal, she left her neighborhood boyfriend and directed her intention toward me. At the time, I felt like the luckiest man in Ohio.

Six months into the relationship, I hoped that our relationship would develop beyond just physical attraction. I struggled with what I was feeling in my heart. The truth inside was in direct conflict with how I was conducting myself in the relationship. This young lady believed our relationship was healthy, but the truth within me was a distraction. The fact was that my heart needed more than J-Lo beauty; I needed to connect with this young lady on a much deeper level. I needed conversation beyond the TV guide or *Wheel of Fortune*.

The one thing that kept me coming back day after day was her two wonderful sons. I enjoyed these two young men so much. When they called me Poppy, it felt natural. It took me a while to realize it was that relationship that drew me to her. I wanted a family, wanted sons of my own. But as much as I was taken by her beauty, I needed more from a woman. I needed that kind of conversation that went beyond the pleasantry of, "How was your day?" I needed someone who excited me, shared the same entrepreneurial spirit I embraced as part of my soul. For her, we were perfect, but, for me, something was missing. As hard as it was, I had to be honest with myself. I was not as shallow as most would think. A pretty face will only hold my interest for so long. But my heart was not committed on the same level as hers was. I could not continue to be a good representation of a man to those young men because I was not truthful with their mother, therefore, I felt it necessary for us to part ways. She deserved someone much better than me. At the end of the day, the best part of that relationship was me being a father to two young men.

I know that, wherever they are today, they are rock stars. When I say, "Be honest from the start," I mean just that. Some time ago, I was emotionally interested in a young lady who seemed from the start to be everything and anything a man could want, and I was lucky enough that she was interested in me. However, as time went on and the layers of who she was began to peel back, I noticed things that made me question why I was still seeing her. Please note, she might have felt the same way because I, too, have my faults. As with any relationship, you must learn to be flexible. From time to time when things come up, and you slap your head over issues that do not make sense, these are the times when you must pay attention to what you can live with long term and what you need to have open conversations about.

Please note, I am not talking about conversations about the toothpaste, the seat being left up or the way you load the dishwasher. I am talking about important issues, the ones you know you should talk about, but you do not. This is because you know how it will end. You will either sugarcoat the issue because you are worried about hurting your partner's feelings or because you find it hard to put the right words together to make your point. The real conversation happens when you are talking to your best friends or the bartender who couldn't care less as long as you're still buying drinks. Somehow, your friend or, worse, the bartender manages to give you advice that sounds worldly and sage at that moment. Once your head clears, you can almost remember what he or she said that made sense when you were pouring your heart out to them. You sit there at the edge of your bed, asking yourself why you keep going back, why you keep taking the calls, why you keep making plans when you know from the start you never intended to include that person? But because you/I felt compelled to do so. Why?

The truth may be that you are too kind. Maybe you are the type of person who always puts the other person's feelings ahead of your own. Or maybe you're a coward, and you hate conflict, so you pray they break up with you. The truth lies within you, in this book, and in the position you are in at this very moment. It is okay to be brutally honest—and you should be—because the person I am speaking to at this very moment is *you*. I dare you to be honest as to who you are before you go out on your next date.

CHAPTER SIX

Needs Versus Wants

After a couple of failed relationships when I was younger, I decided to take a break from dating. My heart could no longer handle disappointment and my head could not take the drama. It was during this dating hiatus that I found myself sitting on an airplane, listening to the inflight instructions. As cliché as it sounds, as the flight attendant described the oxygen mask coming down and specified the importance of putting on one's own oxygen mask before helping anyone else, I finally internalized what I had known intellectually but never grasped emotionally; it is essential to put yourself first.

This may be self-evident to anyone who has done any personal development work, but, for me, one of thirteen kids and a lifelong people-pleaser, grasping this at a soul level has been life-altering and has greatly improved the quality of my relationships.

I discovered that I am important. My hope is, that if you have not already done so, you discover that you are important, too. We all are.

Healthy relationships require both partners to value each other and themselves, and this is where the concept of *needs* versus *wants* is essential. As you embark on your dating trajectory, it is essential that you think about the things you need and the things you want. Some people might prefer a list of "non-negotiables." This can be a useful way to think of it, but I have learned that wants and needs are both important. For example, you might need a mate who is financially secure, open to having children, and honest. No date would make it on your list without these must-haves. But let's say you meet this person and they do not make you laugh or support your dreams or make you want to wrap your arms and legs around them or skip a playoff game to take a walk in the park. That is not a relationship that is likely to last. On the other hand, if financial security, honesty, and having children are essential for you and you meet someone who makes you weak in the knees and has you in stitches but has no job, does not want kids, and is married to someone else and lying to her about you, that will not work either.

Dating With a Full Deck requires being true to yourself before inviting another person into your life. So I am outing myself as a person with needs, wants, and desires, and I am giving you permission to do the same. It is okay; you are the first person in your life you need to fix or save.

Deep down, we all know what we want, but it can be terrifying to be emotionally open to someone else if we make them responsible for putting on our oxygen mask. Conversely, when we acknowledge that we are responsible for taking care of ourselves and are open and honest with ourselves first, it suddenly becomes a lot easier to give and receive love. It is impossible to be loved if you are not *ready* to be loved.

I will give an example from my own dating life. In my first marriage, I had harbored a lot of internal anger toward my ex because I would do things for her while unconsciously expecting her to reciprocate but never feeling I was in a position within myself to be clear about my needs. I would have that conversation only in my head, in hopes that she would acknowledge my attempt to make her needs a priority, and, without being prompted, she would set aside her needs and place a higher value on making my needs a priority.

I had hoped, because of my action toward her, that she would conclude on her own to place my needs over hers. If we are being honest, I know I am not alone here and will say this, for the record this was my fault in not making my needs important enough to have an open and honest conversation about what I was feeling, and thinking my partner would one day come to the conclusion on her own.

It never happened, which is why my second marriage is completely different. We discuss things openly and are even willing to argue as long as we do our best to fight constructively. So neither of us has unmet needs and, most of the time, our wants are being satisfied as well.

Being open to the truth helped me realize that my relationships failed because I either hadn't known or hadn't articulated my authentic self at the beginning of the relationship, and I hadn't asked the essential questions to get to know the other person either. I did a lot of painful self-evaluation. I determined after my divorce that the next person I invited into my life had to want to know me, to value and respect me, and embrace me without trying to change who I am at my core. And, in turn, I had to do the same for them.

Healthy relationships are generative; they promote growth in both partners. But if you pick someone whose needs and values do not align with yours, you're doomed to a stagnant situation and your bucket will never be full.

Emotional healing begins the moment you are ready to be honest with the man or the woman you see in the mirror, and it continues as you allow yourself to be honest with your mate. We spend unnecessary time and energy trying to change ourselves which could be better spent on connecting with others as they are and letting them see who we are, too.

I love talking to people who travel because everyone sees the world in different ways. This planet has so many beautiful places—many are closer than we know. Love is like travel. We invite ourselves to go someplace and experience something incredible and, at the same time, we do not always need to travel far to find what we are searching for. We also want to travel in the style that works for us. Some people prefer hostels over hotels, others prefer fine dining to local cuisine. This translates to relationships as well. You want to find someone with whom you can move through the world, enriching one another's lives and growing together rather than apart.

With every relationship, there will be challenges to overcome, but many of these challenges can be avoided if you are clear about your wants and needs from the outset. The more you let yourself acknowledge the truth about yourself, your needs, and your limitations, the more you can articulate what you want and need with a potential mate.

You must be clear as to what is important to you before you can ask another person what is important to them and before you can be certain if you're prepared to meet their expectations. I know acquiring all this self-awareness is not necessarily "sexy," but we live in a world that is constantly trying to make you think and feel like someone else. You log into Facebook or Instagram and there's immediate and overwhelming input about the highlights of other people's lives.

I have come to believe that the greatest accomplishment one can achieve is to know themselves and to address their own unmet needs. When I first began the process of accurate self-appraisal, I had a hard time acknowledging all aspects of myself without feeling a need to "fix" the things I didn't like, but those efforts to "fix" made it difficult for me to accept that I was lovable even with my imperfections and that others could accept me exactly as I am. At some point, I made the radical choice to accept myself exactly as I am and to do the same for others.

This does not mean I don't value self-improvement. I do. I am a top master level fitness professional here on the east coast, author of a couple of very good books, social activist, entrepreneur, co-host on a podcast, loving father, and coach.

My strengths: I am generous to a fault, idealistic, and I like to think I have a great sense of humor but would make a horrible stand-up comic. My shortcomings: I am very impatient (working on doing better); I have no filter and will say anything no matter how undiplomatic (working on that too); I like my freedom and will run if someone tries to control me or pin me down; I love to be with just one person, love the world and the people in it; traveling excites me; I love the outdoors and dream of a home in the woods where I can sit on the dock and fish in my underwear; I don't like clingy people, mean people, or people who blame their shortcomings on everyone else.

I'm an extrovert, optimistic and enthusiastic, and welcome change. I'm opened to transforming my thoughts into concrete actions and will do anything to achieve my goal without risking hurting someone else. Yes, I'm a true dreamer, and my whole purpose on this earth is to help people embody the best possible versions of themselves.

These changes I help others strive for are not attached to their lovability, worth or capacity to be in a relationship with someone else. I advise all my clients, friends, and loved ones to embrace themselves and their prospective partners exactly as they are and to be upfront about where they are without allowing themselves to descend into the very destructive thought, "I'll be more lovable when I (fill in the blank here)."

Before I ask you to take an honest look at yourself, let me do my own self-evaluation. I am 5'11", athletic, reasonably attractive, somewhat direct and outspoken, a professional risk-taker, romantically needy at times, and torn between my dreams and the world's reality. If I were to go on a date with someone new, I would owe it to them, and to myself, to be upfront about these things and the fact that my ideal mate would be age-appropriate.

Before you start to address your expectations of someone else, first define who you are, then ask yourself what you need from another person. No one can complete you. You must be complete within yourself before you invite another person into your life. That does not mean you have to be perfect, but it does mean you have to know yourself and be capable of taking care of your own needs.

You will NEVER—I repeat, NEVER—find a perfect person, capable of meeting every one of your wants and desires. But you absolutely can find someone you want to build a life with, someone who makes you a better version of yourself but does not try to make you a different person than you are. Let's be honest, even if you found someone "perfect," without any issues or annoying qualities or things that occasionally irk you, that person would not make you happy in the end. Relationships are a pathway to growth. There is no growth without conflict and com-promise.

My grandparents were married for fifty years before finally having a formal wedding with all the typical bells and whistles, including her first and only wedding ring. They were my first living example of true love, and, from them, I learned the value of dedication and commitment. They were not perfect, but, as the saying goes, they were perfectly suited for each other.

I was less lucky in love. I dated one girl from the sixth grade until I was twenty-one. That relationship ended with her infidelity, but I walked away with the best parting gift I could ever ask for—my oldest daughter. After my ex's infidelity, I played the field hard and fast and furious. For several years, I fit the stereotype of a "player." Then, I was married for twenty-two years and then divorced. It took me a long time to figure out what I now know, and what my grandparents taught me by example in being yourself and inviting your partner to be themselves, too. To treat each other with love and understanding, develop a friendship, cultivate romance, and, after fifty years together, you will still want to meet each other at the altar.

My grandparents' official wedding was the wedding most little girls dream of. Not only was the wedding special, but my grandfather also gave my grandmother the ring he could never afford when they first became man and wife. Think about needs over what you want; most want a ring on their finger before the wedding, but how many of you would marry a man on just his word and be just as happy getting your ring fifty years after you said *I do*?

When others learn about what I do for a living most think that I am surrounded by beautiful women all day long with perfect bodies. If I could put a number on those who train at my gym that most would say are perfect, about ten percent on both sides of the gender would label themselves as perfect and or beautiful. However, in my mind, I understand that physical attraction is at the top of most people's needs, more so men, but women are just as sold on looks and six-pack abs on men, and are drawn to those perfectly sculpted bodies.

I'm not sure if it's because of what I do for a living, but, over time in a relationship, looks are overrated. For most men, we must be physically attracted to a woman before we will sleep with them, and most of today's women I come across think more like a man while still trying to hold on to being a woman. If a man is not physically attracted to a woman, she becomes a good friend—unless there is alcohol involved—but in most cases, friends.

Men's and women's needs, from the beginning, are in line with a mutual physical attraction. However, it is the personality that keeps him addicted to a woman, and it's the same for a woman with a guy who is less than a "ten." It is a fact looks will fade with time and age. There is no amount of surgery that will keep a partner's attention if your partner isn't in love with your soul.

Years ago, I trained a couple who had been together for over twenty-five years, childhood sweethearts. The couple—who shall remain nameless, will be referred to as he and she—hired me because she wanted to get back to the body she had when the two had first met. He was okay with how she was, but she was unhappy with how time had faded her good looks; she'd gone from catcalls as she walked by construction workers, to now being invisible no matter how large her cup size was.

In conversations during a session, she would joke about him leaving her for a much younger woman; he'd confirm that his love for her fell far beyond her looks. However, he was most concerned with her addiction to plastic surgery and trying to battle time.

I trained the two of them and, if I must say, I got the two of them in pretty good shape. She had multiple surgeries over this time, and he was very frustrated with each procedure. The more surgeries she had, the more the conversation about her husband leaving her for a younger woman became a reality going into the third year of training the two of them.

The truth is, his leaving had nothing to do with a younger woman. It had more to do with her addiction to returning to her youth. After nursing her through a total facelift, he had seen enough and wanted off this sinking ship. His need for a partner for life could not satisfy her need to be young and beautiful again. Her need to transform herself back to the woman he first met lest she lose him became a self-fulfilling prophecy.

Did he end up with a younger woman? Yes, three years after he left. But the reason for his leaving had nothing to do with age. It had more to do with the fact that his wife was an older woman trying to become something she once was and not celebrating the woman he'd promised to love forever.

Both women and men must understand that looks will fade. You can fight the flab, but you will eventually lose the fight. A relationship that lasts over time has more to do with self-esteem, hobbies, friends, walks in the park, taking care of your body naturally, taking care of each other, and allowing each to morph into a less attractive version of themselves.

When it comes to your needs and wants, no one should ever love and respect you more than you love and respect yourself. The takeaway from this chapter is that a man or a woman who falls madly in love with their partner will start to lose respect, attraction, and feeling for them when their partner does not feel or respect themselves. It is impossible to get someone to fall madly in love with you without them seeing beyond your good looks. Put your partner in a position where they feel lucky to be with you.

CHAPTER SEVEN

The Diamond And The Firefly

I have many my clients who come to me because they want to get off the fitness roller coaster and want to do something that will create a healthy lifestyle with lasting change. They often show up for our first session feeling as if lasting change is impossible but also wanting to keep trying because they know they'll be happier if only they can get and stay healthier. In time, they come to realize that they *can* achieve their goals and are glad they stuck with it. See any parallels to singledom? How many people despair their single status, keep evolving, keep dating, and eventually find lasting love? Too many to count. I, for one, am sure I've known numerous others with similar experiences.

In the gym, my goal is to design exercise programs that fit my clients' lifestyles. If I can help them craft a routine that fits their personality and their needs, they will have no problem sticking with it for the rest of their life.

Dating is no different than implementing a wellness regimen. You must devote yourself to the process to realize results. And if you try an unsustainable approach, you will burn out quickly and, maybe, even permanently. When it comes to anything you want in life, you need to mine for diamonds and stop chasing fireflies.

When I talk about chasing fireflies, I am referring to elusive and temporary results that have no lasting benefit. In the area of health, this might be the equivalent of trying a thousand new diet plans for a day or a week at a time but not sticking to any of them. As far as dating goes, chasing fireflies is going on date after date and having vapid, superficial conversations and never generating a meaningful relationship.

One day, after taking a client through a very intense cardiovascular weight training session, both of us out of breath, exhausted, and slapping each other on the back, I told her, "Anyone can buy you roses but they can't make you feel alive. Only you can do that." My client started to well up at the realization. She is a brilliant and dynamic woman who had suffered for many years with low self-esteem, but over many months of working together, she had begun to believe in herself and to realize that happiness is a deeply personal affair. No one can make us happy. Others can only support us in our journey toward self-fulfillment.

When I finally got out of what friends and family had been telling me was a loveless marriage, I committed not to repeat the many bad habits that had led to an empty and destructive relationship. I looked back over my past behavior and determined that I had been chasing fleeting highs for the entirety of my marriage. I tried to make her happy or myself happy in the moment, as opposed to developing shared values and creating greater space for emotional intimacy.

It took me a while following the emergence from my marriage for me to recognize that I needed to be my own life coach, but once I did, I applied the skills I teach my clients when developing a lasting wellness routine. With my clients, I help them evaluate what does not work and how they've been chasing fireflies (instant gratification with no lasting payoff), and make sure they see that repeating the same actions will generate the same results. Then, once they have the requisite clarity, we focus on the results they want to achieve and devise a plan to help them get there that fits their personality.

If you have not found the love you seek, it's likely because you haven't allowed yourself to be vulnerable and authentic and haven't committed to working on yourself and your potential partnerships. I know this because that is exactly where I found myself. Honesty is a prerequisite for positive and productive action. Once I got honest with myself, I could create a dating plan, the first step of which was *be honest*.

Chasing fireflies will have you behaving like someone you are not because you think the person you are interested in wants you to be different from who you are. We change the way we dress, feign interest in topics that bore us, and go places we do not want to go while pretending we're over the moon to be there. Why? Because we found someone we want to be with. We make the chase more important than the outcome. We think about the now and neglect to concern ourselves with the long-term impact. None of this is constructive and, in fact, it can be incredibly destructive.

Like I told my client, anyone can buy you roses. Anyone can take you to the hottest nightspot or make reservations to an overpriced restaurant where, even after you finish your meal, you are left wanting more. But I do not believe anyone can simultaneously take your breath away and enable you to feel comfortable in your skin. That requires someone special, and it requires you to be that special someone for another.

Like fireflies, people emit an inner light that attracts others to them. But when it comes to dating, this initial attraction has a very short lifespan if it is not accompanied by something more substantial. Do not get me wrong; we need that light. We crave it. I am not saying to investigate the source of the light. Do. But if you notice that the source it is emanating from is flickering and flimsy, run, don't walk, in the opposite direction.

We should never go chasing after fireflies because, if we do, we will certainly lose ourselves in the chase.

As we allow ourselves to reveal who we really are (to ourselves and our partners), we reveal our diamond selves, and diamonds are the opposite of fireflies. Think of your diamond self as the priceless parts of you. These parts never lose their shine unless you choose to dull them or cover them up. Fireflies have a short lifespan, but diamonds last forever. Fireflies are crushed easily and often, but diamonds are created only after the application of pressure over time.

I believe that the best way for men and women to reveal their precious, priceless selves is to immerse themselves in the process of getting to know each other. Be yourself. Be open and honest about your experiences.

I am not saying you should not be on your best behavior in the early days of a relationship, but I *am* saying you should behave like yourself. If you do not believe in traditional gender roles, say that at the outset. If you want children—or do not want children—let that be known. Reveal your deal-breakers early.

Most people start one way, only to reveal six weeks or six months down the road that they are someone other than who they've been pretending to be. This is a setup for failure.

When I talk about working with clients to devise a fitness plan they can incorporate into their lives, I think that process translates extremely well to dating and relationships.

Let's say you want to meet someone. First, you might join a gym because you've been told the gym is a great place to meet hot guys or girls. Smart idea? Not if you hate working out. What about going out on dates and limiting the amount of alcohol you drink, but then leaving each date to meet up with friends and drink until you have to be carried home? This is, obviously, problematic. If you're looking for a serious relationship, not being yourself is your biggest barrier to finding what you say you want.

There is nothing more rewarding than spending time with someone with whom you can be authentic. That doesn't mean you don't want to improve, but improve for yourself, follow your values, as opposed to trying to become the person you think someone else wants you to be.

Without becoming too didactic or preachy, I believe your first date and every date after should reflect who you are. Many of my friends and clients who have found that special someone did so by being themselves. They met playing a sport they love, at the gym, attending a book club, or on an online dating app where they were upfront about their wants and needs.

Be truthful about who you are and what you want. If you have kids, be upfront about that from the outset. If you're an animal lover, share a cat photo on your dating profile. Conversely, if you're allergic to animals or don't want kids, let that be known.

Dating should be fun and positive, and, above all, genuine. So, enter open, honest dialogues from the outset. If you're not ready to talk about a subject, don't, but whatever you do, don't be inauthentic. And, when it comes to getting to know someone else, do not shy away from asking the questions you want answers to. Ask the other person about their values, interests, goals, and past experiences. It's okay to apply a little pressure. Remember, you're looking to cultivate diamonds, not catch fireflies.

When you understand what it takes to create a diamond and how short the life span of a firefly is, and you apply this to dating and or relationships, it will be clear to both sexes that men are different from women. What I have discovered is that women love sex just as much as men, and some more than men. Others are into it, but do not need it on the same level as others. However, men need sex like they need air and will do or say anything to get it. Men like talking about it, "Oh, you have a very sexy voice." I know you have heard that or "You are the sexiest woman I have ever met." Men ask you out at first because they are turned on by you, not because it makes them happy that they now know you have consumed a meal from all the needed food groups for the day. We take you out because we like you, we are turned on by you, and we want to impress you, hoping you will feel the same and want to take the date to another level. But keep in mind, I said *date*, not *relationship*.

To be truthful and fair, women must admit that there of those women out there who have just as strong of a sex drive as most men, but in the case of building a lasting and loving relationship, I would safely say that the woman who is sitting across from you now who is extremely impressed with how you dressed for your date or the car you drive or what you do for a living makes you the perfect family provider. Her primary motivation for being out with you right now is because something about you leads her to believe that you are a diamond in the making.

When I have these conversations with my daughters, as well as young women who are actively dating, I ask them to understand that sex is valuable to men, and please do not make it too easy for a man to get it. On both sides, taking the relationship to the next level is the reward for both of you for all the hard work the two of you had to put in to create a diamond on both sides.

My grandmother would say, "Don't give good sex to a fool who keeps acting out." Meeting doesn't give your most important bargaining chip to a player who acts out and believing that seducing him is a reward or trying to change him will make him fall in love with you. This is a dangerous game you're playing with your heart if you reward his bad behavior when he's not acting the way you'd like. This holds true for women as well.

My grandmother's message, as well as what I have tried to teach my daughters, is that, on either side, if you are looking to create a diamond, never go into a potential relationship playing games because you'll never know if the person you are now out with is a diamond or *not* a diamond in the making.

My best advice to my girl or any woman, is that giving your body to a man who has not earned your love will devalue your stock and have little to no return on your emotional investment.

Giving away your body too soon will, in most cases, decrease your value and will lead to a conversation that "All you want me for is to have sex." In most cases with men, that is true. Even with a man who's a diamond, this statement can be fact at the start because men are taught from the time they come into this world that they are warriors, and warriors like to conquer things. That's the reason a man's status in the workplace is so important to him. So, a great way to keep his interest is to make him work for it. I didn't say *play games* because that's just crazy and you risk turning a diamond into a stone. The point I am trying to make here is, to keep your partner interested, you both must put in the work before defining the physical part of the relationship.

Even though I was taught that men are different from women and that we are wired differently, I believe that, outside of the difference in hardware, that both sexes have been rewired, and the gap that once made each sex different has been changed by what is, today, called "media economics."

My best advice is to understand that even the firefly wants to be a diamond, but a diamond is created over time. Each person needs to put in the hard work before the creation of a rock becomes a precious stone we long for and admire. Remember in the dark of a summer night, the flicker of the light from a firefly is short-lived, but a diamond is created over time. Diamonds are forever, so it is up to you to chase the fireflies if that's what you're into, but keep in mind that, to create a diamond, you must put time and work in on that stone, chipping away at the layers, learning everything you can about every layer of this rock. The more you peel back, the more you learn about the stone. With the right amount of work in getting to understand that stone over time, even the wildest of fireflies can become a diamond if the firefly is open to changing the natural way it flies.

When I was playing organized sports, we would call the short-lived relationships "Saturday night specials." We'd meet on Friday, stay over until Sunday, then went back on Monday, all the while saying we would call on Tuesday, Wednesday, Thursday, and Friday... but never did. The "Saturday Night Special" was the one thing I looked forward to the most.

Everyone loves a firefly, but a diamond is forever.

CHAPTER EIGHT

"The One" Or "The One For Now"

I used to coach high school and college track and field. As a coach, I saw my role as to be there for my athletes physically, mentally, and emotionally. One day while I was coaching after school, standing by the bleachers, watching my runners take a few cooldown laps before ending the practice for the day, my eyes caught a smiley-faced young lady walking toward me. I recognized her immediately as someone I had coached several years before and, when she approached, she said she was there to observe the team and see if I was still coaching.

We engaged in the requisite small talk, exchanging pleasantries, then I introduced her to the team before dismissing them for the day. After the team left, my former athlete and I sat on the bleachers, and I asked her to tell me more about what she'd been up to in the years since we'd last seen each other.

Like many college graduates, she was finding it difficult to find a job in her field. She told me she was planning to relocate to see if there were better options elsewhere. As I listened to her, I couldn't help but think about how, once upon a time, I'd packed all my belongings and moved as far away from my hometown as I could. I told the young woman I supported her decision to explore the world outside of Phoenixville, PA. However, I did question if a better job was the real reason for her desire to relocate.

In my experience, people make drastic changes for two reasons: they are either running toward something or running away from something, with the hope that something in their life will get better. I asked her if her intended move was motivated by love, and her reply confirmed my suspicions. When I heard her story, I was immediately struck by how heartbreaking it is when a person doesn't value themselves.

Here's what was happening: my former athlete had been seeing a young man for almost two years. He lived just outside of New York City. According to her, because of his work, the relationship had always been on his terms. She explained that he was so immersed in work that he had very little time for her. He'd reach out at his convenience and, love-struck, she'd drop whatever she was doing to drive more than two hours from one state to another to see him.

She knew, deep in her gut, that she wasn't this guy's priority, but she'd been telling herself that, one day, he'd see her as "The One."

I asked her, "After two years, have you met either his mother or father?"

She replied, "No, but he told me I'd meet them one day when the time is right." She went on to say, "I know he loves me in his own way. He just has trouble saying he loves me."

It did not make sense for me to tiptoe around what I already knew. "If I can be honest," I said, "there are two classifications a man puts a woman in. She is either The One, or she is The One for Right Now." Please know, this does not only apply to men; it applies to women as well. Women have their terminology for "right now." They call it The Friend Zone. This means a woman likes someone enough to keep them around. Meanwhile, that person hangs on to the hope that, someday, she will see them as more than just a friend. The keyword here is *friend*. Always marry your best friend, right?

Being "The One" is completely different from being "The One for Now" and it is often easier to see this from the outside than it is to see and acknowledge it from within.

The young woman was beautiful, talented, kind, and committed. She deserved better than she was getting from a man who saw her as disposable, but she did not know her value. Because of this, she wasted time, money, and energy on a selfish, entitled guy. It turned out that, when she told him her plans to move, instead of asking her to stay or making plans to visit, he wished her good luck and goodbye. Although she was devastated at the time, the end of this relationship turned out to be the beginning of her journey to self-worth.

I told my former athlete, "As a woman, you are in control of the dynamic of any kind of relationship you get into. To get a man to respect you, you must demand respect from the start. A woman must know her value from "Hello." Pay attention to how you carry yourself, how you speak, the company you keep, and how you articulate what you want and what you need."

While that relationship (which was not much of a relationship, but more of what I have heard referred to as a "situation-ship") failed, I followed up with the young woman. I discovered that, after a brief period of devastation, she went on to do some much-needed inner work, and when it came time to date again, she demanded respect from the start. She has since gone on to meet and marry a great guy. When looking back at her entitled ex, she doesn't know why she wasted her time on him.

A major problem in early dating is that people don't want to risk losing the object of their interest, so they'll often make sacrifices that aren't in their best interests. This is a huge mistake. If you find yourself being the one putting forth all the effort, that's a problem. I don't advise playing games or making people "chase" you, but you don't want to make it so easy for your prospective partner that they start to take you for granted.

Men and women fall in love differently and the way they demonstrate their affection can never be compared. When a woman makes up her mind that you are The One, she will be your cheerleader, your ally, your therapist, your friend, your coach, and your confidant. Men aren't as versatile. But we're also not that complicated. If we want to be with you, we'll let you know. We'll introduce you to our friends and family, talk about a shared future together, and do our best to keep you close and lock you down. When a man knows your value, a man will walk over fire to prove to you that he wants to be with you.

If a man isn't taking steps to let you and everyone else know he wants to be with you, he sees you as his "for now" not his "forever" and if a woman doesn't see a future with you, she'll treat you like an afterthought and not prioritize you.

No matter how you want to look at it, there are only two categories that a man or woman will put you in. You are either The One for Right Now, meaning the relationship is disposable and/or convenient, or you are The One, meaning that they want to do what they can to secure a lasting future with you.

Don't be fooled. When people first meet, the thing that interests them is almost always physical attraction. This is especially true nowadays in the swipe-right world of online love. But if a man is worth his salt, he won't be content with a happy meal or a pop-up; he'll want a full thanksgiving dinner. And if a woman believes you could be her forever person, she won't text you at ten p.m. when she's bored and has nothing else to do.

When you begin to date from a place of abundance and self-worth, you'll naturally value and respect yourself. You'll refuse to be someone's afterthought when you could be their priority. An important thing to note is that there is a huge difference between self-care and selfishness. If you are looking for The One, it's important to remain committed to practicing self-care and making sure that you're meeting your emotional needs from a variety of different places and not relying unfairly on one person to be your sun, moon, and stars. On the other hand, relationships are, by definition, relational. Therefore, you want to be considerate to the one you're with and find someone who will do the same for you.

In short, don't be like my former athlete. Don't chase after someone who doesn't want to be caught. Even if you catch them, the cost of doing so will likely be losing your sense of self-worth.

As much as I would like to solely direct this chapter toward my female readers, I must direct the words on these pages toward the few men who will take the time to turn more than ten pages in this book.

Times have changed, the dynamic of dating has shifted between the sexes. Although a woman must know her worth, her actions must support the conversation and interaction with her male counterpart.

In today's dating market, sex is always on the table at some point. But, if your date is interested in you beyond the closed door or the back seat of your BMW, both sexes need to get the best return on their investment (ROI) to get between the sheets. The person will one day wake up next to you, and go above and beyond to become more to you. If you make yourself too easy to sleep with, it will also be just as easy to leave you with only a text or a posted note, letting you know that they have grown bored with you.

A person who is into you (both women and men) will stand with you and support your goals, provide and protect you, have conversations for the future that include you, will include you as a featured person to their dream, and drop whatever they are doing at the moment to care for you when you are sick. A person who wants you to be The One will leave you important clues. If you are a slow learner, when your partner tells his or her friends publicly that their life is better with you, it will be clear to you and everyone else around you that you are The One and not just for right now, but forever.

CHAPTER NINE

Love At First... Touch, Sight, Smell, Kiss

Have you ever touched someone's hand and wished you never had to let go? Have you ever hugged someone and wished they would never let you go? Have you ever met someone you immediately wanted to be with forever?

Not everyone will experience the intoxicating rush of love at first (fill in the blank), but those who have often follow their story of initial attraction with tales of drama and devastation. There are, however, occasionally times when this initial spark translates into life-long lasting love.

Years ago, before Uber and Lyft, Carl, a limo driver, got a 2 a.m. called to pick up a high-profile passenger. He pulled up to the circular driveway around the giant call letters of a TV show and waited for about a half-hour. When the studio's doors finally opened, the woman who emerged was only about five feet tall and, yet, as far as Carl was concerned, she was expansive. Carl jumped from the car to introduce himself and, as she reached for the car door, he grabbed her hand to stop her. She looked at him with a "What the f---?" expression, but Carl quickly explained that opening the door for her was his job. He also told her that, where he comes from, men treat women with reverence and respect.

Tanya smiled, took a step back, and allowed Carl to open the door for her.

This was a chance meeting of two people from two different parts of the world. Carl was a working man with a strong work ethic and high standards for himself. Tanya was a TV star, seemingly living the dream.

That one night turned into Carl driving her for the next six months. She went from just riding in the back of the limo to demanding that she ride in the passenger seat so she could look at Carl as they talked on the ride home.

Not too long after he started driving her, Tanya had a July 4th cookout at her house and invited Carl to the celebration. Although Carl initially declined the invitation because he didn't feel comfortable with her circle of friends and the difference in their economic status, Tanya convinced him to come. He accepted her invite but was reluctant to bring a plus-one because his current relationship was being stressed by his new friendship with Tanya. Carl tried to explain to his girlfriend that Tanya's dating circle read like a *Fortune* magazine's "Most Successful Men in the Business" article, but the woman he was dating was jealous and didn't believe he and his employer had a working relationship and nothing more.

In the end, Carl went to the cookout alone, and when he pulled up to Tanya's hillside mansion in his freshly detailed twenty-five-year-old used Porsche, Tanya greeted him with a hug that would change the course of their relationship forever. The two shared an extended hug. Tanya held onto Carl as if she never wanted to let him go. Carl whispered, "I will give you a week to let go." Tanya whispered back, "Can we make it two?" When they finally did release each other, they gazed deep into each other's eyes and had the best time ever at the party.

Days later, Tanya called Carl to pick her up but said she didn't want to get picked up in the limo. The call came in after midnight and she was being picked up from an address where Carl had never picked her up or dropped her off before. By the time he arrived at the address, it had started to rain.

A very wet Tanya hopped into his car. The hour-long drive to Tanya's house was mostly silent. Tanya curled up, shivering in the bucket seat of his car.

When they reached her house, Carl started to get out to walk around and open her door, but Tanya quickly jumped out of the car and started running toward her house. The heel to her shoe broke and she turned her ankle. Carl responded by picking her up and carrying her to her garage door. Still, in his arms, she entered the security code and, once inside, Tanya insisted he stay. Both were soaked. Carl put her down and she limped upstairs to change into something dry while he waited in her kitchen, soaked. Minutes later, Tanya walked into the kitchen in a very plush white robe with a white towel wrapped around her wet hair. She asked Carl if he wanted anything, and he replied that he wanted to make sure she was all right before he left. Seeing that Carl was soaked from head to toe, she insisted he remove his clothes so she could dry them. Not taking *no* for an answer, Tanya brought him a matching white robe and he retired to the powder room to change.

The two sat on her loveseat, then Tanya curled up in a ball and began to cry. Carl put his arm around her and held her. She had, it turned out, just gone through a very painful breakup and Carl was there to support and love her as a friend.

The friendship held strong for more than twenty years. It overcame countless failed relationships on her part, and two marriages on Carl's end. Holding back his true feelings for Tanya was excruciating for Carl, and two months before his second marriage, he sent Tanya a message announcing that he was about to get married. Carl was looking for a lifeline, wanting to tell his best friend how madly in love he was with her. He was hoping for a *Pretty Woman* moment, but that moment never happened. Carl stood there on his wedding day, scanning the crowd, hoping that Tanya would show up and stop him from making the second biggest mistake of his life. Tanya never showed and Carl married, only to discover that his new bride had been having a two-year affair that continued well into their marriage.

Carl, broken-hearted, was at a point in life where he considered giving up on any chance of finding "happily ever after" when he got a text from Tanya, asking him to help her move some things from her old home to her new home. Without any reservations, Carl showed up to help.

As the two unpacked her belongings, Tanya asked why Carl had never asked her out. He replied by taking both her hands into his, looking into her eyes, and telling her that he had not been honest with her over the years. He said that, when he'd sent the invitation to his wedding, he'd been looking for an opening to tell her how he felt about her. He said he'd stood there on his wedding day, hoping when the minister asked if anyone had any reason this marriage shouldn't happen, she would've stood up and stopped the wedding.

He also told her that he didn't want to lose her as a friend, but that he could not continue life without letting her know that any time he was near her, his heart skipped a beat.

In reply, Tanya kissed Carl. Not a romantic kiss. A gentle kiss. Her lips to his, she pulled away and simply said, "Thank you."

Two years passed from that moment, and one day, out of the blue, Carl got a text from Tanya that read, "Don't want you to leave this world and not let you know that I have always been in love with you. Thank you for loving me for who I am. I couldn't give you what you wanted, because I didn't want to hurt the first and only man who loved me for me, but I need you to know I've always wanted you."

Neither Carl nor Tanya ever acted on that text or the loving sentiment beneath it. To the outside world, they are good friends and nothing else, but the two of them will always know, within their hearts, that they want to be together.

You may be wondering about the point of this tragic yet heartwarming tale. The point is that love does not necessarily equate with compatibility. It is possible to be intensely attracted to someone and not have what it takes to make a relationship work. When it comes to dating, the most essential thing you can do is work through whatever barriers exist within you that would lead you to sabotage the possibility of love. Tanya didn't believe herself worthy of a healthy and loving relationship, and Carl settled because he was afraid to express his heart's true desires.

I would encourage you to continue to develop the capacity to let love in and to be opened to taking the risk, not just of feeling love but of taking the necessary actions to fan its flickering flames. Keep in mind, a fire does not exist just to burn stuff down. Fires burn because they provide heat to keep our souls warm.

Sometimes, even when you know all the rules, no matter what is on your list, there is always a force much greater than anything that experts can write or research. Sometimes, you must trust your gut—nine times out of ten, your gut is always right.

Over my career, I have met and talked with countless numbers of people from both sexes who were waiting for Mr. or Mrs. Right to come around. No matter who you are and where you are in life, we are all hoping that the next person who enters our personal space will have their stuff together.

We have become so jaded that we might not notice love when it presents itself in our lives. While we work overtime and are distracted by our busy lives, we continue to pick the wrong people. Love can be magical if you're open to receiving the gift. We talk about opposite attractions, and it's true. However, it doesn't mean that it's a good thing. Everyone you see together is not meant to be together. Sometimes, the one you are meant to be with may be with another. Note, I am not telling or advising anyone to break up a perfectly good relationship from the sideline, but I am not advising anyone to stay in a situation when your heart and mind are telling you that you should escape.

Life today is much like the afterlife; you are either going to live a heavenly, loving relationship or you will live your life dying and describing that life as a living hell.

None of us can help whom we are attracted to, it's true.

The heart is like the highway; sometimes it takes you where you want to go at just the right speed or you get on the superhighway with your foot pressed to the floorboards, going at world-record speed, zooming past every patrol officer parked on the side of the road. Or you get off course, taking side roads of emotion, redirecting your heart from the love you long for to love for right now. At the end of the day, each road reaches an intersection, and if you just keep driving, your heart will be presented with choices.

Grandma used to say that opposites attract, but she also said that, when you flip over one magnet, the force that once was pulling everything together can break when the polarity changes. No matter how close you try to push them together, there are forces beyond your control that will keep you apart. You can never make one plus one equal two when you're not good at math or a good person. You have to start in a good place within your own heart before you welcome in another. I will leave it up to you to determine how much you understand of what my grandma said because, at the end of the day, it's what's true to you that matters.

In one of my day jobs as a professional fitness instructor, I am privy to some conversations that normally don't come out in an early meeting with a mental health professional. Why? I'm not sure, but like hairdressers and barbers, we tend to have more open and meaningful conversations without biases or judgment.

I have said many times that the first man or woman we learn to love is our parents. So, if a person grows up with a codependent parent or in a home where love is unsure and unpredictable, they most likely will end up in a relationship with a narcissist person or one who is manipulative and treats them badly. This is all because of the love language they learned at home.

By nature, most of us seem to go for a partner who seems familiar—"my type"—which is the reason most people find themselves going from one bad relationship to another. We all have a *type*—until we finally get enough and want *off* the emotional rollercoaster and begin to rediscover a new love language.

None of us can say our upbringing was as perfect as the life we are living today. Most of our dating issues stem from our childhood, and the others stem from us wanting more from love than we received growing up.

Which leaves me to ask, "Do you believe in love at first sight or not?" Does your subconscious heart know what your conscious heart wants and needs? So, I will leave it up to you to believe if love at first sight is possible or not, but if your heart skips a beat when you sit next to or hug a stranger, do you walk away without saying hello?

Who knows what gift God just gave you?

Chapter Ten

Something You Should Know About Me

Before I had kids, I used to think I was willing to risk (and therefore, potentially *lose*) everything to "have it all" with someone. I thought finding a soulmate was worth letting go of everything else that mattered to me. Now I know that the only way to find someone worthy of building a life with is to hold true to one's values.

When it comes to dating, dreams are important, but even more important are the actions we take to deliver on what we say we want. If we want to share our lives with someone, we must be intentional about what that life will entail, and we owe it to ourselves to be upfront about our expectations and abilities.

Growing up, it didn't dawn on me just how little my family had until I started seeing the larger world and being exposed to the way others lived. I learned what it felt like to want more out of life and began setting goals and taking steps to achieve them. Dreams are funny. They can either motivate a person to do more with their life, raising the bar for someone else to follow, or they can be nothing more than empty, unrealized wishes.

I'm not saying we must chart a forever plan on every first date, but I *am* saying that we can't be prepared to abandon our life goals just because someone we don't yet know has a winning smile, our biological clocks are ticking, or we tell ourselves this is our last chance at love.

Dating With A Full Deck requires being upfront about our wants, needs, and desires. Yes, this is an emotional risk, but it's a bigger risk to abandon ourselves for the illusion of love. I know that more than anyone.

At 2:15 p.m. on August 22, 2013, I drove my car into my garage, closed the automatic door behind me, and sat in my car, not wanting to go inside. I dug my phone out of the center console and began to call all the people I deemed important. I was in a dark place, yet, out of the thirty-three phone calls I made that day, only my oldest daughter and my youngest son asked me if I was okay. The others chatted with me about the details of their lives but didn't once say, "And, Kevin, how are you?"

I placed my phone down on the armrest, put my seat back to its reclined position, closed my eyes and prayed. I told God I was tired of living, asked Him to forgive my sins, and implored Him to welcome me home. It was only as I began to request that He look over my children that I scrolled through their photos on my phone and thought about the promise I'd made at their birth to provide and protect them. I decided at that moment that I couldn't just die. I had to live; I had unfinished business in this life. Although I was experiencing intense emotional anguish and was unwilling to live for myself, I couldn't intentionally leave my children since I knew that would scar them for life, damaging them from growing close to anyone in fear that they would leave them without question.

I realized that day, after the failure of my marriage and my decision to choose life, that I had ended up desperate and suicidal because I'd been chasing my ex for decades but hadn't been true to myself or my needs. I'd wasted a lot of time and energy by trying to be someone I wasn't, and, in the end, I'd ended up miserable and alone.

I made a vow to myself that day that I would never again lose myself for romantic love. No. I needed to come to every new potential relationship from a place of fullness, without expecting the other person to fill the voids inside me and without placing all my hopes on them. I also knew in that instant that anyone I dated in the future would have to know that the most important things to me are, and always will be, my children and my faith.

I vowed that, on my next first date, I'd let the object of my interest know the things that mattered to me, and I would never again hide behind my mask of machismo.

Shame and Blame are two horrible relatives. They come to visit and refuse to leave no matter how much you subtly hint that they're not welcome. But the reality is, we invite them in by failing to accept ourselves as we are and by hiding our true selves from others. When I called those thirty-three people that day, I continued to maintain my façade. Even suicidal-level depressed, I couldn't bring myself to open up.

No wonder my marriage failed. I didn't know how to be me, and I felt completely alone even when surrounded by people.

Looking back, I am still trying to figure out which one of us overlooked our flaws or were we both blind to our incompatibilities?

The key to finding love is to stop trying to find—and to *be*—a flawless partner and, instead, to meet someone with similar values and goals with whom you are compatible. Perfection is an illusion anyway. Not only that, but it's also boring. Have you ever met someone who came across as completely two-dimensional and flawless? If so, you probably felt you couldn't connect with that person at all. If you're like me, you were annoyed by them.

A strong relationship consists of two imperfect, like-minded people who can sustain a life together. It requires a certain amount of routine and monotony. That's not to say successful relationships don't thrive off infusions of newness (and, ideally, a whole lot of laughter), but you must be able to be yourself with a partner to maintain your sanity and your relationship.

A person who embraces his or her true self will be better prepared to love someone else.

As part of the process of dating, you want to be open about your perceived faults and failures. When we try to hide our vulnerabilities, we end up seeming stuck-up and disingenuous. I invite you to be yourself from the beginning. If you're messy and disorganized or chronically fifteen minutes late, say so. If you don't know the difference between GAP and Gucci, don't show up dressed to the nines or suggest a first date at a fashion gala. Be yourself and you'll uncover if you are compatible with the person you are getting to know. If I had done that the first time around, I never would have found myself in a marriage that brought out the worst in both myself and my ex-wife, and I never would have ended up alone in a garage, praying for a way out.

I don't regret the past at all. I am grateful for the lessons I learned from that relationship, the wonderful children my ex and I had together, and the place I ended up in life. I am happier with myself. What I am saying is that the way out of lovelessness is being yourself, whoever you are. I learned that the hard way, but you don't have to.

Looking back on my first marriage, I only saw her best side when we were just dating, and I am sure she would say I only revealed the same to her—which, I would like to say, was as real as I could get. However, once we moved in together, bad habits, mood swings, personality traits that made it difficult to deal with her flaws, my flaws revealed themselves, and as much as we both tried, over time, it got worse.

To the outside world, we painted a pretty picture. We were both trying to get over our shortcomings and live happily ever after.

I have asked myself what I would have done differently, or what could I have done to be a better husband and partner. Was I so lovesick that I was blind to the things that drove us apart? Was I so far gone and wanting a family of my own, that I put up with things I later learned I could not deal with? Maybe I was afraid to be alone and thought this was the best I was going to get. Maybe I oversold myself with the promises of things I was going to do and could not deliver within a timeframe conducive to paying our family bills on schedule. Maybe the dream of spending the rest of our life together wasn't as good an idea once we both got a closer view of what our lives were.

Please don't get me wrong, we were together for twenty-two years, and some of those years were great, but knowing what I know now—and knowing how it ended—I ask myself if I would do it again. She might say *no*, but I would say *yes*. Not all of those twenty-two years, but most of them.

For years I was asked to change, and for years I didn't understand what I needed to change. I tried and failed because what I had to give up also made me unhappy, and if I had given up on what brought me the most happiness, you would never learn anything from any of the other books I have written.

It is true that we all are looking for the best from a potential partner, and, sometimes, the picture we paint to draw another in is not authentically presented.

If you take nothing else away from this chapter, remember that none of us, at the start, sees past our date's shortcomings because we are first looking for *potential*. The blindness to those shortcomings comes from the dream of being together forever.

The desire to be madly in love makes both sexes blind. The fear of being forever alone leads us to take unusual emotional risks, and the promise of potential does not always have space on your timeline.

Come to this date with full disclosure and allow your date to know as much about you without putting yourself in a predicament that your date will feel the need to go all UFC on you.

CHAPTER ELEVEN

Pride And Prejudice

We are born into family systems, social circles, and cultural norms. Our thinking is shaped by personal experiences and ancestral histories. It follows, therefore, that we are taught things about love and hate. These lessons become embedded within us and, if left unexamined, we will continue to harbor beliefs that don't serve us. Wars have been fought over religious beliefs, sexual orientations, racial and cultural disputes, economics, and all manner of prejudice. And, on a more personal level, relationships have been destroyed over political and bigoted points of view.

There is no divorcing the past from the present. Looking at our past is essential for moving forward into the future we hope to create, and, for most, we are not the person today that we were yesterday.

There is not one person on this earth who can claim to be a hundred percent without some sort of prejudice. I say this because it's important to acknowledge that the biggest barrier to agreeing to disagree with a potential partner is believing that you are right, and they are wrong. This leads people who might be compatible to enter power struggles that create toxic relationships or prevent people from entering relationships at all.

Generally, we put too much value on what other people think and how we believe they will judge us. In dating, it can feel easier to make blanket judgements against others without taking the time to get to know who the other person is. The more we can suspend our preconceptions, the more likely it will be for us to authentically connect with someone else.

During my research for this book, I interviewed hundreds of men and women about how their past experiences have shaped their perceptions of the present. It came as no great surprise that many people who'd been hurt in the past had internalized assumptions based on their experiences. They said things like "all men are dogs," "women are crazy," and "all the good ones are taken."

I have been on the receiving end of these types of broad generalizations and, if I'm being entirely upfront, I have likewise made assumptions about others that turned out not to be true. I remember, when I first entered the dating world after my divorce, being set up with a female divorce attorney in my town. Having just gotten a divorce and still smarting, I unfairly projected my past pain onto the present and, suffice it to say, the date with the lawyer did not go well.

When it comes to achieving success in any relationship, be it business, parenting, dating, marriage or even managing your interactions with an ex, we owe it to ourselves and each other to take responsibility for our failures. Don't misunderstand this. By no means am I giving you license to berate yourself or feel guilty. But ownership is essential. Taking responsibility for the things you did or didn't do that contributed to the demise of a relationship is essential.

We all like to believe it's someone else's fault when we aren't happy, but until we take responsibility for our unhappiness, we can't take responsibility for our happiness.

Your interpretation of what happened in past relationships will either create a highway toward happiness or an alleyway to misery.

We are all individuals and that's what makes each of us so special and each of our interpretations so subjective. No matter where you are from or what you've been through, you've been influenced by this world, and you've influenced it. Your voice matters. So let yourself share your opinions but know that they are just that: opinions.

I have been told that we should never talk about religion or politics in social settings, especially on dates, but, for many people, politics and/or faith determine how they see life, what they value, and what they want for themselves and their loved ones. If you're a devout person or an atheist or something in between and your faith, or lack thereof, matters to you, be upfront about that. If you're a staunch Republican or a diehard Democrat, share about that, too. The last thing you want is to find yourself in a relationship with someone whose values threaten yours. That's a setup for failure. That's not to say people of differing faiths or opposite political perspectives can't build meaningful lives together; they absolutely can—but only if they can agree to disagree. So, share what you value and see if the other person can value you enough to respect your point of view, and vice versa. You want to respect the one you're with even when you disagree with them.

I've discovered that the most successful relationships aren't devoid of disagreements. They are full of them. No two people think the same and, in a true partnership, each person will hold their views and exhibit their values. One of the successful components of a healthy relationship is the ability of each partner to agree to disagree.

My interpretations and perceptions of God may be correct or not, but I can't be with someone who makes me appear wrong for what I think and how I feel. I can, of course, open myself to the opinions of others, but I can't subvert my perspective just to keep the peace. Realizing this early on in my post-divorce dating life led me to disclose my faith early on and, to my surprise, it was one of the things that made my wife fall in love with me. She told me soon after we became exclusive that she valued my adherence to my values.

Strangely, one of the things that made me fall for her was that she voiced her opinions, even when they differed from mine. I realized that she was someone who knew the importance of honesty, and the trust we developed between us has only led to a deepening of love.

Reveal your core values to your date. Step outside of your prejudices and pride to learn about their views with an open mind and a receptive heart.

I used to have a friend with whom I cut ties years ago based on her repeated voicing of a perspective about same-sex marriages that I found impossible to reconcile within myself. This friend believes homosexuality is not blessed by God. The more she voiced this point of view, the more I realized I couldn't have her in my life. I tried to get this friend to understand that we live in a different world from that of our Bible forbearers and to encourage her to expand her point of view, but she never would, and that became an ongoing point of contention between us.

It didn't matter how highly I thought of her as a friend in certain areas, her prejudices made our friendship untenable.

If you're a churchgoing person and you discover that the person you have just asked out does not share the same commitment to religion as you do, this is one of those issues that could be a problem or a dealbreaker, depending on your perception of what your date believes. Know your date's position on a topic and be sure to share yours, too.

The fifty-four cards that accompany this book are designed to encourage a fun, non-judgmental, open dialogue. If you look at dating as the best game you'll ever play, the one where the stakes matter and the only real rule is "be yourself," then not only will you win in the end, but you'll also achieve win after win along the way. I know it's cliché, but the worst thing you can lose is yourself.

Don't go looking for a person who will become your loan officer, bodyguard, babysitter, trophy, chef or maid. If that's your aim, you'll only be left feeling empty in the end. Put yourself in a position to find a partner to share a life worth living. Raise your dating IQ. To do that, you'll need to communicate honestly from the outset. This starts with the small things and transcends to the big ones.

I've polled countless people about dating etiquette, and I can't begin to tell you how many men and women have walked away from what they thought was a great date with someone who promised to call only to never hear from the other person again. If I had a dollar for every time I heard this, I'd be a rich man.

Although this practice (commonly referred to as "ghosting") is unfair, it speaks to the lack of authenticity that is considered allowable today. My challenge to you is to resolve to mean what you say and say what you mean, and let your actions support what you say. Invite your date to be upfront. Let them know that you value feedback and make it safe for them to be open with you.

It's good to enter dating with a willingness to learn from the process. Learning means being willing to be uncomfortable. Notice patterns in your dating life. If someone tells you they're not interested, have the courage to ask them why. If more than one person raises the same issues, that's valuable feedback.

There are hundreds of reasons why people don't make it past the first date, but you want to think about whether you're valuing quantity or quality. Better to have fewer dates with like-minded people with whom you could see a future than a date every night of the week with little chance of any of them leading to lasting love.

There is nothing anyone can put into a book that will direct you to how to pull off the perfect first date, but an honest conversation is a good place to start and will provide an excellent foundation for you to continue.

I once had a client who told me about meeting a phenomenal man while at the park. This client was there walking her neighbor's dog and when the man came up to pet the dog, assuming it was hers, not only did she not correct his misconception, but she also perpetuated the illusion. They exchanged numbers and dated for a few weeks and eventually broke up because, when she finally told him about the dog story, he felt she couldn't be trusted. He was right. She'd told him half a dozen other harmless untruths to make herself seem more desirable. My client was so convinced no one would love her for herself that she refused to let anyone see the real her and alienated quite a few potential partners who might've liked her if she'd dared to be authentic.

When going on a date, you certainly don't want to come across like you're conducting a job interview, but you do want to be on the lookout for your potential partner's prejudices and strongly held perspectives. You want to share your truth and create a safe space for them to do the same. I advise people to embrace, rather than avoid, occasional moments of dating awkwardness. Treat each first date like you would a conversation with a friend. Enter authentic dialogue and, chances are, you'll end up wanting to see the person again—or not, in which case, better to discover that you're not compatible sooner rather than after you're already invested.

As I've grown older and have looked back on my many relationships and dating mistakes, I have learned that I trust too easily, need to be more honest with myself, to step out of denial, and to see people and things more clearly for what they are.

One of my biggest flaws is I worry about hurting other people's feelings, and I put up with some people just because I cannot say to them, "Why are you in my life?" I have a friend I've known for years who, in conversations, is extremely transparent about wanting our friendship to be more than just friends. I do not have the heart to flatly tell her *no* for fear of hurting her feelings. So much so, that each time she calls, I hesitate to answer the phone because I know the conversation will lack the substance I so enjoy from others who are living a more fulfilling and meaningful lives. She is a good person with a good heart; she just isn't the person I see myself waking up to Sunday morning and having a meaningful conversation with over breakfast. Plus, no matter what the conversation, she always interrupts me with her issues that have nothing to do with the conversation. I always stop whatever point I'm making and say to her, "Let's just talk about you." She's not a good listener nor does she bring much to the conversation—nor to the relationship, not that there could ever be one. But please don't get me wrong, it's me, not her.

The truth is, she's a good person and I like her as a friend. I'm not attracted to her on a physical level nor do I connect with her intellectually. The one thing I will say that I just hate is the way she answers the phone, "Yo, what's up?" On my end of the call, the sound is like nails on a blackboard, but that's on me, not her.

I know for many of you that are reading this will say, "Why don't you just tell her you're not interested in her that way, and let her know you'll never be any more than just friends," or share with her that I was doing battle emotionally with another that I was still trying to disconnect from.

Yes, part of human behavior is sometimes not always sharing all the intimate details of every facet of our lives with everyone our paths may cross, and yes, you would be right. I should, and in so many words I have said that, but, at the same time, I *didn't* say it. I stayed in the neighborhood of saying it, but never actually said those words—but, as I said, one of my many flaws is that I don't like hurting anyone's feelings, but I guess in not telling her, I was doing just what I am trying to avoid doing.

In every encounter of the heart, there will be those points that need to be made and conversations that need to be had. To get comfortable you must be uncomfortable first.

In 2020, an election year, the country was more divided than it'd ever been, and this put stress on the conversations people might have wanted to have but avoided because they were worried or concerned how the other person would view them.

I witnessed a father refusing to pay for his child's education because she posted a picture of herself on social media protesting for human rights, which he strongly disagreed with, believing that she'd been "taught better than that."

Denying your feelings and hoping a person will change will only add stress to the relationship you are hoping to build, but allowing the person you're planning to go out with or date know, going into the relationship, that you aren't really into football on the level your date is or pretending to be a world-class foody when you're a beer-and-nuts kind of person is disingenuous and inauthentic. There is not one person who loves everything or everyone, and there is not one person on this planet who will invest quality time with a person who hates everything and everyone. However, there are some people that can self-adjust because someone gave them a good reason to.

As people, we have two options: "Chance" or "Choice." We can take the *chance* to learn or like some new, or we can stay in our lane and let life happen to us, take no risk, and live our lives as we have always done with the same outcome. "Our Choice" is no risk, no reward. The point here is, if you are open to changing your behavior or stepping outside your comfort zone, that thing you thought was a deal breaker may not be such a big deal with the right person. Being with you is risking, and adding someone else into the mix is just as risky, but isn't this the reason we live this life, to take chances?

Maybe turning over a card from this book will open the door to an honest conversation between two good people, maybe friends who could be more than just good friends.

CHAPTER TWELVE
No! And Hell No!

If we are honest with ourselves, we are all emotionally damaged. I don't say that to be negative. Acknowledging the brokenness that exists inside us can be an irresistible invitation to lasting intimacy. Let me pave the way. I was abandoned by my mother and had an emotionally absent father. I grew up feeling as if the people I loved could disappear at any time, and I tried to do whatever I could to keep love in my life—up to and including lying to people about my mother's abandonment so they wouldn't suspect what I thought I knew—that I was so unworthy that even my mother didn't love me enough to stay.

I've come a long way since the misperceptions I developed early on in life, but my ability to shift out of that way of thinking and believing only came about after I had a series of reparative experiences, all of which required me to be intimate and honest.

Knowing a person's insecurities and being able to communicate our own is important. You want to share more than the highlights of your life with a potential significant other. You also want to share your fears and insecurities.

Honestly, had I understood the ways my childhood experiences had impacted me, I would never have married my ex-wife. I'd have realized that our relationship dynamic was one of always chasing after one another. That wasn't a healthy dynamic for someone with my background.

Due to the wounds I experienced early on in life, I require a partner who is reliable and available—physically and emotionally. Also due to the wounds I experienced early in life, I am loyal to a fault, have trouble handling emotional outbursts, and sometimes override my wants and needs to keep the peace. Knowing all of this equips me with a powerful internal compass toward the kind of relationships that work for me—like the relationship I've evolved into with my current partner.

Sometimes when embarking on a new relationship, people are tempted to go for what they *want* as opposed to what they *need*. That's not to say we can't have both but start with what you know you need and build from there. For example, in the past, I dated CEOs and captains of industry, powerful professional women with a lot going for them. Many of these women were phenomenal individuals, but they were also extremely independent, no-nonsense, and apt to abandon their relationships and lose themselves in their careers. None of them was a good fit for me and I, a needy dreamer, wasn't good for them. Had I acknowledged this truth earlier, it would have spared me a lot of heartache, but I kept going for what I thought I should go for as opposed to what my mind knew I needed and what, ultimately, filled my heart and helped repair the wounds of my past.

We can't rewrite history, but we can do our best to find relationships that don't constantly activate the pain of our pasts. Whatever messages we receive about love early and often will only be reinforced if we find ourselves going for people who remind us of our parents and/or those who raised us. If you had a healthy childhood and unconditional love and support, try your best to replicate that as an adult, but if you didn't, let yourself choose from a place of love and logic, and don't let yourself settle for a repeat of your past.

By now, I'm sure you've worked out that *Dating With A Full Deck* is about accepting and embracing the truth. The greatest emotional prison a person can live in is the prison of dishonesty. Dishonesty need not always be overt or intentional. Sometimes, it can be unintentional. We lie to ourselves. At the risk of being obvious, lying to ourselves about someone in whom we are interested becomes more tempting when sex enters the equation.

I have no monopoly on morality, and I believe that everyone is entitled to engage in whatever sexual activity they want with whomever wants them in return. Plus, I would be remiss if I did not point out that sex can be a highly charged experience and it can be tempting to excuse and overlook certain fundamental incompatibilities once you have had a dose of vitamin-O.

Sex is natural and desire is inevitable. There is nothing wrong with wanting to have sex. That said, people experience attraction on different levels and physical intimacy impacts them differently.

If you want to be physically close with someone, be upfront about what that means to you and what you expect because of that connection.

Sex can complicate things in the best and worst ways possible. And, when engaged in too early, those complications can prove problematic, and possibly unresolvable.

For most people, the first several dates are fact-finding missions rather than potential opportunities for intimacy, but keep dating long enough, and sex will come up. My suggestion is not to go down the intimacy path without talking about it. If you're ready for sex, you're ready for a conversation about it. After all, the act of making love is about much more than simply biology. It's about the interpretations and emotions that accompany it, interpretations that differ from one individual to the next.

There is nothing wrong with having sex and there's nothing wrong with *not* having sex. But whatever you decide to do (and whenever you decide to do it), you want to be open with yourself and with the other person.

We human beings damage each other in innumerable ways. We can start to become more aware of red flags only by asking questions we might deem forward or impolite and challenging ourselves to get to know the real person rather than settling for an obvious façade.

I've learned over the course of my personal and professional experiences that some people ought to come with warning signs. "Beware of the dog!" "Stay away!" "Don't enter!" "Proceed with caution!" "Crazy is my middle name." "Everything is about me!" "I have very little going on, but I am cute!" I could go on, but I won't; you get the idea.

During dates, make mental notes. Be attuned to both what is and what *isn't* being said. You cannot change the events of your past, but you can change the trajectory of your future by learning from your previous patterns and adapting your behavior accordingly. If, in the past, you had sex with an ex and then became completely enamored, know that pattern is likely to repeat itself. If you avoided intimacy and never felt close, watch out for that moving forward.

The only constant in your relationships (past, present, and future) is *you*. So be sure to adapt, evolve, learn, and grow. The right relationship will free your soul from the destructive patterns of the past. This doesn't mean another person can save us—they can't. But we can save ourselves by not going after people who will only keep us entrenched in our brokenness. Know that we are all human and all imperfect and, at the same time, it is possible to find someone who fits you like a glove.

I've always found it interesting when people say, "He's a good catch" or "She's a good catch." I don't see people as fish to be caught or released. I see them as sitting alongside you in the boat, helping you cast your line and reeling in a life worth living.

When you focus on your priorities and are true to yourself, your ability to love and be loved increases. Be consistent. Don't try to reel anyone in just for the sake of "catching" them.

Relationships aren't as complicated as we make them out to be. Be consistent with how you feel, stay true to your word, respect your partner's time and space, and talk through important topics and issues. Understand that no one has the same heart as you and be honest to a fault. Let your date know if it takes you four hours to get ready or if your kids sometimes drive you crazy or if you swear like a sailor. And talk about sex before you have it, and even during and after. Communication is a gateway to intimacy, and the more you can express what you want, in and out of the bedroom, the more likely it is that you'll achieve moments of absolute ecstasy and a whole lot of joy along the way.

Chapter Thirteen
Swipe Left, Swipe Right

When I began to outline *Dating With A Full Deck*, I didn't want to delve into the topic of online dating. I knew so many people who had experienced horror stories when meeting strangers online that I had become more than a little skeptical. Yet, when it came down to it, I also could not overlook the reality that many people are using online dating platforms to find love. You would be hard-pressed to find a single person nowadays who has never been or isn't currently on a dating website.

Today's couplings are a lot like fast-food restaurants. They're all about convenience. I'm not suggesting that there's anything inherently wrong with online dating apps or that people don't appreciate intimacy, but I do believe we have to work against our impulses for instant results if we have any hope of creating enduring relationships.

We human beings are incredibly innovative. We've figured out ways to fast-track our educations, our careers, and our modern-day conveniences. The days of working a forty-plus hour workweek and retiring with a pension and a gold watch are behind us. Rather than seeing life as a marathon, we view it as a sprint—running all-out toward what we want and wishing we could have it yesterday.

We live in a world in which we are told that we have unlimited options, and this can be detrimental to us in the long run. It should go without saying that, when it comes to developing a serious relationship, your partner must become a priority and not another option that you can "swipe left or swipe right." This means committing to working through issues that arise. It means acknowledging that your search for something "better" may cost you in the end.

In my profession, I hear a lot of stories about couples breaking up over sexual infidelity and, most of the time, the unfaithful person ends up regretting their choice to look elsewhere. They say things like, "I made a stupid mistake" or "I didn't know what I had until I lost it."

How do you decide if you've met the person you want to commit to? I can't tell you that. What I *can* tell you is that commitment is a surer path to happiness than swiping people out of your life based on impulsivity and instant gratification. When it comes to online dating, I believe that attraction is important, but values matter more. If you see someone you find intriguing and their profile meets with what you're looking for, swipe right, but don't feel you have to explore all potential options or you're likely to explore yourself out of something that has the potential to be phenomenal.

There is a big divide between the world I grew up in and the world that is awaiting my kids. Dating sites like Match.com, eHarmony, OkCupid, and Tinder have turned getting to know one another into getting over one another. "Netflix and chill" pass for quality time. But does it? While writing this chapter, I turned to the experts: my college-aged son and his best friend.

I asked them about their experiences with various dating sites. My son didn't want to talk to me about his swiping experiences, but his best friend had found a committed relationship on Tinder. He told me he was exclusive and in love, yet, when I asked him if he'd come off Tinder, he said *no*. His girlfriend had, but he hadn't. When I asked him why, he said he liked looking at the pictures, but she'd stopped because she got bored.

The more my son's friend spoke about the details of his online dating experiences, the more I began to understand why he had trouble letting go.

Dating sites are designed to pique our curiosity and make us feel as if we have unlimited options. They incite our attraction and our desire and offer an outlet for our impulses. I asked my son's friend if his girlfriend knew he hadn't deleted Tinder. She did and, according to him, she didn't care that he kept the app and occasionally looked through it when he was restless or bored. Although I'm not so sure I'd feel equally okay if I were in her shoes, I can say without a shadow of a doubt that this level of transparency between them is a sign of the health of their relationship.

When I embarked on this writing project, I discovered more about the human psyche than I ever wanted to know. I have decades of experience helping people transform their minds and bodies through incremental effort over time and a commitment to their goals, but writing requires a different level of questioning about other people's ideals. I knew from my years working with others that when people take a committed approach to their goals, they achieve results that last. When they set out to achieve instant results with fast-track strategies, they tend to end up disappointed in the long run. This has proven the same for relationships. But the more I talked to people in and out of relationships, the more I began to understand why so many people experience problems in their modern relationships.

If we look back through the history of marriage, we see an entire body of evidence that demonstrates that the less we devote ourselves to the process and the more we focus on the results, the higher the divorce rates, the more people end up single, and the less likely we are to achieve dating and relationship longevity.

My opinion may be dated, but it's also based on experience. If you're looking for a lasting relationship, you can absolutely find a partner online but, once you meet them, you can't continue to behave as if you can swipe away any incompatibility.

More options do not mean better options.

Love is not about finding someone who matches some perfect image in your mind. It's about finding someone you want to share a life with and with whom you can be honest and accountable. Love is an invitation to grow as a person and the only way to do that is to invest in the process of mutual exploration. That can't be achieved by continually longing for something other than who, or what's, in front of you.

Dating sites can, themselves, become a metaphor for an unhappy relationship. As long as people believe there's something better out there, it will always be a swipe left or swipe right culture. If you are quick to dismiss one person in favor of another or get bored easily or don't invest the time to review a person's profile, you're likely to end up with superficial and surface connections.

If you are single and want a lasting relationship, cultivate the capacity to stay after you've swiped. This begins by taking a quality-over-quantity approach to dating. Sure, you can swipe and swipe and swipe, but be intentional. I've met people who opt to swipe right on every single profile because they've developed an "I'll talk to anyone interested" attitude. This practice isn't fair to them or their potential partners.

There's a saying that I like a lot: "How you do one thing is how you do everything." If you want a quality relationship, be a quality dater. Invest in exploring compatibility even from the outset. Be who you are. That doesn't mean don't select photos that show off your best assets, but it does mean don't post photos from ten years and thirty pounds ago. Don't lie about your height or say you're looking for something other than what you want. The best thing you can do is be your authentic self and select people with whom you might be compatible.

Often, we crave the quick fix of instant gratification and a momentary high, yet studies suggest that the greatest happiness there is comes from adhering to our values and taking actions that support our goals. It's the people who surround us and the choices we make that bring us the most joy. When you are true to yourself, you are setting the stage for ongoing happiness and authentic connection.

People don't wake up in the morning and say to themselves, "I am going to make myself miserable today." Yet, our pursuit of momentary payoffs and instant results tend to leave us feeling empty in the end. All of us know at a basic, intrinsic level, the actions that are more likely to yield positive results in the end. I encourage you to take the time to get honest with yourself about the actions you've been taking that haven't been leading to the relationships you seek. Then commit to stopping them. If you're agreeing to dates with people you know you're not interested in, settling for scraps, or anything else that's destined to leave you alone and lonely (or with the wrong person, which is also a surefire recipe for loneliness), you're not being true to yourself. You have the power to keep kissing frogs or to start looking for princes or princesses. I encourage you to choose the more rewarding path.

I am learning that dating is very expensive for those who don't have the time, or the emotional wherewithal, to strike up a meaningful conversation with someone they are interested in. I have a friend who has spent up to three thousand dollars on a dating site just to have lunch with someone who shares a similar bank account balance. None of them are perfect and finding a person to spend time with should not come from a catalog of physically beautiful and successful people. I am old school. The person next door or the person I meet in the hardware store works just fine for me.

CHAPTER FOURTEEN
To Be Or Not To Be, That Is The Question

The more I began to study various relationships and what did and didn't work about them, the more I realized that the word *be* is of infinite importance. We must decide whether or not we want to *be* with another person. We must figure out what things we should let *be* and what things require intervention. We must *be* with the one we're with, and not continue to search elsewhere. Most importantly, we must *be* ourselves.

There are no tricks or magic pills that will make you more marketable to the opposite sex. Instead of striving or doing, we are, more often than not, better off *being*.

Every day we attend to our personal needs and sustain ourselves, every time we allow ourselves to be where we are without trying to immediately alter a situation, we are putting ourselves in a position to honestly evaluate what *is*. It's a lot like meditation.

In case it's not obvious from my writing style, I've been diagnosed with ADHD. My mind tends to flit around, and I've had to work very hard to manage my impulses to be everywhere other than in the here and now. Because the skill of *being* doesn't come naturally to me, cultivating it has been even more meaningful. I've discovered that it's important to practice simplicity in dating and in life. That means not trying to become something I'm not. I've learned that authenticity is far more rewarding than striving for perfection.

When you go on your next date, remember that the person who you asked out, or who asked you out, is excited about spending time with you. The *real* you. But that can only happen if you let yourself *be*.

Every date is an opportunity to slow down, connect, and experience the moment, moment by moment. The value of that cannot be overestimated. Some people will advise you to make every date exciting, but I'll advise you against that. I've known people who were so excited by each date itself that they didn't take the time to accurately assess their excitement in another person. For example, going to a concert for a date might be fun and exciting, but it's not exactly a great venue to chat with someone new about their hopes, dreams, and ideas.

Do not invite someone over for dinner for a first date, or even a second one. It gives the impression that more than dinner is on the table and, as mentioned earlier, having sex too early accelerates relationships in a way that can cloud your judgment or prevent you from accurately getting to know the person you're interested in. Dinner at a good restaurant, a picnic in the park, coffee, or a walk are all great ways to connect. That doesn't mean you can't do something fun or innovative. How about painting pottery or horseback riding or working out together or some other fun activity? As long as you go somewhere where you can talk and learn about each other, go for it. But make sure not to confuse the fun of the activity with your feelings about the person doing it with you. And don't agree to an activity you know you'll hate. If you're not a gym person, don't suggest working out. If you are a dedicated meat-eater, don't opt for a vegan restaurant. Set realistic expectations early and often.

Let your date see you in your element and do your best to do the same with them. That way, you'll quickly discover your level of compatibility—or lack thereof.

One night, while celebrating one of my son's seventeenth birthday, my family and I were at the Cheesecake Factory for dinner when we found ourselves seated next to a couple out on a first date.

Because the adjacent table was uncomfortably close, we could see and hear everything that was happening, and their date proved to be the entertainment of the evening. Not only were both the man and woman texting on their cell phones and paying only partial attention to each other, but within the first twenty minutes of their arrival, the guy called his date Debbie, Deborah, Donna, and then Carol. It should be noted that none of these names was her actual name. After his fourth mistake, the woman informed him, loudly enough for our entire section of the restaurant to hear, that her name was "Suzanne."

Although this example is unusually atrocious and most people practice better dating etiquette, it illustrates a phenomenon that is all too common: not giving the person we're with our undivided attention. It is important that you are focused on the person you are out with and not on your phone. It's also important that you treat them like the unique and engaging individuals they are. This includes learning their name as well as other details about their life. As if the man at the Cheesecake Factory wasn't badly behaved enough already with the texting and incorrect name-calling, it got even worse.

Outside of not remembering his date's name, he repeatedly made attempts to touch her. I believe that touching a person too soon and without an invitation is a violation of their space and could potentially be a turnoff. Trying to touch someone who you've been devaluing repeatedly is even more egregious. It objectifies and dehumanizes them.

Let's be clear. It's reasonable to touch, flirt, kiss, and anything else you want to do with another consenting adult on a date—but *only* if they consent to it. It's good practice for both people to agree to physical contact before initiating it and it ought to be a prerequisite for physical intimacy that you at least respect the other person enough to call them by their name (unless you've agreed to use aliases as some fun couple's role-play). For all the men out there, remember that a woman must be comfortable with you before she is willing to engage in any physical contact. It must be an unwritten rule and be understood as the law that a woman is in one hundred percent control of whatever happens before, during, and after a date. So, unless she explicitly lets you know that physical contact is desired, don't presume. And know that if she's open to a gentle touch of the arm, handholding, a peck on the cheek, or even an impassioned make-out session, that doesn't mean you should sprint to the car to retrieve the overnight bag you packed "just in case." The goal of dating isn't to get to home plate. It's to win the long game, and the only way to do that is to be yourself, be respectful, and get to know your potential partner. Enjoy the process.

How? Glad you asked. It all circles back to that simple word *be*.

The advice I outline in *Dating With A Full Deck* is a lot like the advice I give my fitness clients. It might not be especially sexy—no shortcuts or instant gratification—but it's solid and it'll pay off, not only in the long-term, but throughout the process as well.

Let yourself enjoy dating. Smile about it before, during, and after each date. A smile has a profound effect on how you feel and how others feel around you.

Your smile is your brand—meaning, how people see you. It is a positive sign that lets other people know they can relax around you. Plus, a smile is painless. It costs you nothing to give, but, like love, every time you give it away, you get more in return. I'm not saying force yourself to pretend to be or feel anything you aren't. I am saying that the more positive you are about life and the more you surround yourself with others who make you feel it's okay to be yourself, the greater the likelihood of finding someone you'll enjoy spending time with.

Don't date out of desperation and don't look for someone to complete you. You don't have to be in a relationship because of your age, social circle, real or imagined flaws or anything else. Relax and enjoy your dating experiences the same way you'd enjoy time spent with a friend.

People need to stop looking for someone else to fill in whatever voids they might be experiencing. The sooner we can accept and embrace our voids exactly as they are, the easier it becomes to see our wants and needs. Also, when we stop looking for someone else to complete us, we become capable of setting boundaries with others. Healthy relationships require boundaries.

Be respectful and mean what you say. Keep your eyes on the person in front of you, pay attention, and be upfront. If you didn't enjoy a date, don't promise to call or say, "We have to do this again." Practice saying *no* and when you say *yes* it will be much more authentic, even to yourself.

Allow yourself a chance to get to know the person sitting across from you. Pay attention and be attentive. The success or failure of a date will depend upon the little things, the tiny moments of connection, or the realization that there isn't enough between the two of you to justify the additional exploration. You made enough of an impression, whether through physical attraction, conversational chemistry or something else to get to a first date, so be yourself and see where that takes you.

Disclaimer: no date is ever perfect, just as no one is ever perfect.

You don't have to get every detail right to move forward along your intended path to a committed relationship.

If every man behaved on a date like a man they'd want their daughter going out with, and if every woman treated a man's heart with the same tender care she'd hope a woman would offer her son, this world would be filled with many more successful relationships.

A positive attitude will attract positive people to you. And let's skip the small talk. That doesn't mean you can't mention the weather but try asking the other person about their favorite season or what they do when it's raining. Talk about experiences and find opportunities to evoke the imagination. Don't worry too much about the topics of conversation, as the cards that accompany this book will provide a springboard into a meaningful and memorable conversation.

Learn all you can about the one you're with. The more you know about the life the other person is leading, the more you'll be able to see yourself as part of it or know if it's not a good fit overall.

A tiny tip that makes a world of difference is to be nice to your servers and strangers.

When you are not nice to other people, you convey an attitude of cruelty, intolerance, and an ego that is a surefire turnoff. One of my clients told me about going on a date with a man who berated their waiter, and even though he was great in every other way, she never saw him again and I didn't blame her. You can't fall in love on the first date, but you can fall out of love—and quickly.

Keep your conversations light but be honest. Think about your reasons for asking this person out or agreeing to the date. Put away your cell phone and commit to the path of commitment.

If you are dating and looking for a lasting relationship, you don't have to demand exclusivity on date number one, but you do want to know whether the person you're with is looking for The One or for The One Right Now. For a variety of reasons, a lot of people have no interest in a connection beyond a few weeks or months. Get to know a person's intentions. They'll tell you with their words and show you with their actions.

Listen. From the beginning and forever. It can be all too tempting to listen to what someone else is saying only so we can tell them what we are thinking, rather than opening ourselves to the possibility of seeing where someone else is coming from.

There is no way to create a comprehensive list of dating *Do*s and *Don't*s but the one dating nonnegotiable should always be to be your authentic self.

CHAPTER FIFTEEN

Only Time Will Tell—The Timeline

Remember the saying that good things come to those who wait? My brother modified the adage, repeatedly saying, "Things come sooner to those who take." I don't believe either of those is entirely accurate. When it comes to dating, we can't hold others hostage without severe consequences. *Taking* will only get you so far and it might even get you arrested. On the other hand, we also can't sit around hoping and wishing or we'll end up wishing ourselves into our old age, single and still wondering why we never found The One.

I've come to believe that preparing for a quality relationship is a lot like planning for a great vacation. It's important to know what you do and don't want, to do a little research, to use your past experiences to determine where you'd like to go, to put money aside, and set up your life so you can devote the necessary time to live the experience, and know that the best things that happen on your trip will be the things you couldn't plan for in advance.

To illustrate this point further, I sometimes use the analogy of a trip across the country. If I'm in Pennsylvania and I want to go to California, I need to know my intended direction if I have any hope of getting where I want to go. A lot of people will say things like, "Dating is a numbers game," but is it? I don't think that's entirely accurate. If I want to get to California and I'm starting in Pennsylvania, heading north or south won't get me any closer to where I want to be. It's the same with looking for a prospective partner. All momentum is not created equal. If you want to end up in a committed relationship, a slew of one-night stands won't get you there. If you want to get married and have children, dating someone who doesn't want kids will only turn your biological stopwatch into an alarm clock.

Even in matters of the heart, we must be smart, thoughtful, and strategic.

In my relationship with my first wife, I was very thoughtful, though not always smart, or strategic. I can still recall a time early in our marriage when I stopped at a New York City florist to purchase roses for my then-wife. When the florist asked about the occasion, I responded that I wanted my wife to know I was thinking about her. His response surprised me.

With a wink and a smile, the florist told me that if I genuinely cared for my wife, giving her everyday red roses was ordinary and unoriginal. He told me that if my love was genuine, I should consider giving her sterling silver roses. He went on to explain that giving this type of rose conveyed a clear message that I would be pledging my undying loyalty and love. Like the catch line of *Jerry McGuire,* "You had me at hello," this guy had me at *roses*. Of course, I ordered the sterling silver ones to make the biggest, most enduring, statement. The salesman's words were a reminder of the importance I placed on love and on being the man my then-wife deserved.

I filled her office with one dozen long stem sterling silver roses plus nine dozen of the everyday red roses, booked a suite at the Hilton Hotel, ordered lunch with grapes, cheese, and champagne, and stood out in the rain at a payphone across the street from her office (in the days before cell phones) to invite her to lunch just as the roses were being delivered.

If someone is important to you, you must make your feelings and intentions clear. The sterling silver roses were part of the process of developing a meaningful relationship. I will always value the time I spent with my ex, but, in retrospect, I can say that I should have bought her roses, rented a hotel room, gotten champagne, then taken the time to connect with her soul. I didn't do that. I saw my California (my intended destination) as marriage rather than on finding and maintaining soulmate-quality love. Had I known what I know now, I'd have had more authentic conversations, sooner and more often.

To develop a truly meaningful relationship, you must be willing to be functional and not merely flashy. Every time I walk into the grocery store, the checkout lanes are filled with magazines shouting the latest news in celebrity break-ups. A lot of people wonder why the rich and famous have marital strife. I don't. I know from experience and observation that love can only be sustained over time if the attraction is deeper than a surface, or purely sexual, connection.

When two people meet, timing is important but so are timelines. If one is ready for a relationship and the other isn't, don't try to force it. When there is an emotional connection between both parties and the relationship is growing at a natural pace without pressure, it is much more likely to last.

You don't necessarily want a rigid pre-set timeline, but you need to know, in a general way, what you want and when or you're destined for a power struggle. That's not to say these things can't be negotiated, but if you want marriage within a year and you're dating an avowed bachelor/bachelorette who breaks out in hives at the very notion of exclusivity, run, don't walk, in the opposite direction.

When it comes to timelines, there are no right or wrong options, but there are right and wrong for you as well as for your potential partner. There are deal-breakers in terms of beliefs and values. If the person you're seeing requires sex within a couple of dates and you want to wait until marriage, that's a deal-breaker. Ditto if you expect a marriage proposal after six months and they're on the six-year-to-the-altar plan.

Everyone's timeline is different, so you don't need to find someone whose destination matches yours exactly, but you're looking for compatibility. Don't ever sacrifice your values or your vision.

We all know what situations will be workable and which will only hurt us in the end. That doesn't mean we have the capacity to foretell the future, but we can read the writing on the wall. We can ascertain if someone is fundamentally incompatible. Don't think that, if you tell the other person what you want, you'll drive them away. You might if they're the wrong person, but that wouldn't be a bad thing. Think about yourself. If you're looking for *forever* and someone tells you they're looking for the same, that will be an inducement to keep moving forward, but if they tell you they're looking for a hookup, you're likely to end things. That's as it should be. *Dating With A Full Deck* requires us to head for our intended destination without settling or compromising our ultimate intentions.

Never forget that there are billions of people in the world so you have options. This isn't to say you want to swipe your way out of finding your soulmate, but to acknowledge that the kind of thinking that holds that there is only one person with whom you can build a future is just as dangerous as treating each potential person as if he or she is disposable. You're looking to get to your intended destination—a like-minded person with compatible hopes, dreams, and goals—in a timeline that works for both of you. Your timeline matters but don't become so focused on it that you'll slot anyone into your life because you want your future to look a certain way. I've known quite a lot of people who ended up divorced or in unhappy marriages because they met their partners at a time when they "felt ready" to be married and opted to commit themselves to the next person they met without taking the time to assess if the other person was someone with whom they could build something lasting.

To continue with our early analogy of taking a trip, have a sense of where you want to go, but know that the destination is less important than the journey. If you're like me, you've had the experience of traveling somewhere exceptional with someone you weren't at all excited about and had a less than stellar experience when, on the other hand, you could travel somewhere so-so with an exceptional person and have the time of your life. So, create a map, set your course in that direction, and be flexible while, at the same time, proceeding forward in a self-honoring way.

Chapter Sixteen

Really? Everyone Gets A Trophy?

I live in a small town in Pennsylvania where our youth sports programs have been designed by supportive parents who believe that every child should get the same amount of playing time, no matter their skill level. Likewise, in these leagues, at the end of the season, everyone gets a trophy. At most of the games, no one keeps score. Intellectually, I understand the reasoning behind this way of thinking and acting. It makes sense to me that parents want their kids to feel as if they matter. Yet, in practice, this way of evening the proverbial playing field has the unintended consequence of teaching children that, no matter the effort expended or the skill set, they are entitled to a certain (winning) outcome.

When the season ends, the star player and the one who spent every game studying their belly button receive the same reward. If we apply this type of thinking to adult life, we run the risk of believing we are entitled to a quality relationship no matter what we do or don't do or how much or how little of ourselves we invest in our search for a loving and lasting relationship. Fantasy blurs reality. We lose sight of the fact that, in the quest for love, showing up isn't enough. We must invest. I do believe there's a lid for every pot. We don't have to be perfect to find a quality match and forge a meaningful relationship; we do, however, need to expend effort.

When I was growing up, only the best kids played and those who lacked the requisite talent learned to work hard or, at the very least, how to support from the sidelines. Entitlement wasn't rewarded. Far from it. Everyone didn't get a trophy. Those who got one had to earn it, which made it much more meaningful in the end.

It's the same with romantic relationships. If you want a lifetime of love and connection, you must be prepared to do more than show up and expect to "find" love. You need to be willing to practice hard and often, to give your all to the game, to lose on occasion, and to keep coming back and evolving. Anyone I have worked with or known who has created a lasting, loving relationship has made it clear that they've expended quite a lot of effort. My grandparents were together more than fifty years before my grandfather passed in 2008, and they were just as in love at the end as they'd been at the beginning. And if you're thinking that's because they were a natural and effortless fit, nothing could be further from the truth. They grew together, worked at their relationship together, told each other hard truths, and were invested in improving both individually and as a couple, never once did I ever hear either say one was doing more than the other. When you care for your partner on such a deep level, there is no need to keep score.

When my sons Alex, Theo, and Connor played in one of these supposedly non-competitive, equal-opportunity sports leagues, I asked them if they found playing fun given that there was no winner or loser. My son, Alex, looked at me like I'd lost my mind. "Dad," he said, "we know who wins and who loses. We're all keeping score."

The biggest secret of the league was that the kids weren't fooled by their parents' illusions. They knew if their team was winning, and they valued an earned trophy far more than a gratuitous one. Similarly, as the years went on, the kids who played hard and put in the effort continued to progress in their chosen sport while the others lost interest and abandoned the game in favor of other activities.

The art of dating is just as competitive as a varsity or professional sport. There are winners, there are those who sit on the sidelines, and there are losers. Unlike a sports competition, however, there are an infinite number of ways to lose the dating game. Losing happens when a person neglects their legitimate needs, pursues their illegitimate wants, settles for an abusive or inattentive partner, or fails to date at all despite wanting lasting love. Sitting on the sidelines is like not dating at all, as is only going out with people who choose you even if you're not interested in them.

What, you may be wondering, *does winning look like?*

In a dating context, winning is sticking to one's goals and values and going for a relationship with someone with whom you share chemistry and compatibility.

When it comes to dating, there is someone for everyone, but the someone for you can only be found if you go after what you want. Don't just settle for convenience or short-term happiness. Think about playing the long game.

Now, more than ever, we have the capacity to find what we seek provided we're willing to do the work. We are in the midst of a sexual revolution. No matter what a person's proclivities, they can find someone who shares their sexual and emotional desires. It's a great time, full of options and outlets. But, for some reason, people seem to be invested in finding sexual compatibility while forgetting about relationship compatibility. I see sex as a short-term win. A goal scored. A temporary excitement. One of my most memorable moments as a sports spectator was sitting on the sidelines during a children's basketball game in which one young player got the ball, dribbled to the hoop, and scored. Only problem? The kid shot the ball into his own team's basket!

Dating these days can feel a lot like that. People get so excited by their forward momentum that they fail to realize they're heading in the wrong direction and scoring in opposition to their interests. Or their refusal to keep score and the "everybody wins" mentality can keep them from investing in their relationship's future.

Today, sending an 11 p.m. text message for a hook-up passes as courtship, and ghosting is seen as a dating rite of passage. It's abysmal. When it comes down to matters of the heart, dysfunction is mistaken for romance. No thank you. It is time to look beyond superficial wants and develop a clear vision as to what we need and desire from ourselves and our relationships.

When I found myself newly single at fifty-four, I decided to take a serious and self-searching look at the many mistakes I'd made in my past relationships. Like many people, I'd made irresponsible and shortsighted decisions that led to dysfunction, carnage, and depression.

My fear of being alone or being rejected led me to seek out meaningless partnerships. I felt even more alone within my couplings than I'd have felt if I'd let myself be alone and wait for more compatible connections. I disconnected from my needs and pursued my wants in ways that didn't serve me.

I have come to find out (the hard way) that, when dating, it is essential to be self-aware and to control yourself enough to forgo temporary gains in service of your ultimate goal. There's another parallel in the sports and fitness world that might be useful to consider. If you want to live longer, feel good in your body, and be proud of the image you see in the mirror, opting for the temporary satisfaction of a cigarette, a Big Mac, and a weekend spent lazing on the couch won't serve you. Going for a walk, drinking lots of water, and enjoying green leafy vegetables will. In fitness and relationships, you want to go for what's healthy and fulfilling. There are no special prizes for starvation and self-deprivation, but you should avoid destructive indulgences because they will only hurt you in the end.

If what you have been doing in the past has not worked for you, you must take ownership of your mistakes and shortcomings and change your behaviors. Gaining control over your actions and reactions can be achieved with just a little effort and awareness. Define the changes you would like to make and develop a strategy to execute those changes. Your ultimate end game is to be happy in this life, find solace in a relationship, and achieve peace and prosperity.

Looking back now, I am quite sure that if I had been open and honest with myself and my ex-wife from the outset, either we never would have gotten married, or our marriage would still be intact today. I didn't try to be deceitful, but I wasn't *dating with a full deck*. I was coming to my relationship having forfeited my cards in advance. I valued someone else's feelings and needs over my own to such an extent that I couldn't have articulated who I was or what I stood for.

I have come to believe that codependency and narcissism are two of the greatest evils in romantic relationships. The more we lose ourselves in trying to make others happy, and the more we expect others to do for us to the detriment of themselves, the more incapable we become of having a true and long-lasting partnership.

Like a lot of people, I am a hard-wired people-pleaser. While growing up, I learned to avoid conflict at all costs by sacrificing myself for the wants and whims of those around me. While these strategies worked well for my childlike self, I carried them into my adult relationships and could not figure out why I ended up feeling devalued and unloved.

Whatever your tendencies are regarding relationships, they come from somewhere. But the past does not need to define the present. Life is a perpetual process of reinvention and rediscovery.

My personal goal is to embrace who I am now, deliberately modify the coping strategies that no longer serve me, and make better choices moving forward. That's all we can do as human beings: seek out a partner that will complement your lifestyle, appreciate what you bring to the table, and encourage you to give and take within the relationship, and be committed to doing the same for them.

If you continue to hold onto the youth sports team philosophy that everyone wins and everyone is entitled to a trophy, you're denying your sense of responsibility for the work you put into life and leaving the results you get out of your efforts up to the whim of fate. True empowerment comes only when we can *own* our actions and our outcomes. I'm not saying that we're responsible for everything that happens to us, but we are responsible for our actions and reactions.

The game of life is simple. There will always be someone with a better body, more financial success, and more talent. None of those matters. What matters is that you give your all to life and play the game effectively. If you find someone you both love *and* like, who finds you funny, looks forward to hearing your stories, wants to see you at the end of the day, and if you feel like your relationship brings out the best, most authentic, you, then you're a winner. Sustained happiness is the most rewarding trophy we can receive and it will come if we work for it.

Recently, I was scrolling through my Facebook notifications, and I saw that a friend of mine had posted about his kids getting two-giant trophies just for being part of a team. My friend is a competitive person, so I wasn't surprised when I read his reflections on the issue of his children's unearned trophies. He said he was going to put both trophies away until his kids do something to earn them. He also said he wanted to teach his kids to assess themselves and their efforts accurately. I found myself not only liking and commenting but silently cheering in my seat. I do not doubt that his kids will earn those trophies. The surge of pride that accompanies the moment when he gives them the awards they deserve will make receiving them well worth the wait.

CHAPTER SEVENTEEN

The Hero's Journey

When I finally worked up the nerve to tell my family and friends that I was getting a divorce, I was surprised to discover they weren't surprised.

A few members of my inner circle said they'd known I'd been unhappy for years. Others said they didn't see what my ex and I shared, beyond the kids who were now grown. The most impactful response I received came from one good friend who sent me an email. The most striking line of the email was, *as you look back on your life, you will realize that every time you thought you were being rejected by someone you thought was good for you, you were being redirected toward someone better.*

I like to think about each person's journey to finding lasting love as akin to the well-known trope of the hero's journey. If you're not familiar with the term "hero's journey," you've no doubt seen and experienced it in movies, books, and any other storytelling forms. Many modern-day, quest-based video games replicate the hero's journey trope.

The path of the hero is as follows:

1. The story begins with a flawed and ordinary individual.
2. That individual is faced with adversity and given a challenge he/she needs to overcome.
3. After first resisting the call to overcome adversity, the hero finds allies and begins a journey that is full of trials and tests, littered with setbacks, but, ultimately, causes them to evolve.
4. The hero continues to press forward and is rewarded with personal growth and other achievements or material gains.
5. The hero returns home after having transformed and evolved because of his/her experiences.

If you navigate your relationships with the hero's journey in mind, you will look at failed relationships as part of your path to lasting and successful love.

After some much-needed time to lick my post-marital wounds, I decided that I would become the hero of my journey to love. I was, and am, a flawed person who had faced and was continuing to face a wide range of challenges (an ordinary individual), but I knew that to embark on the extraordinary journey to love, I would need to evolve.

Like most successful men, I am attracted to strong, independent, kind women. I don't need a partner to cook or clean for me. I can do those things for myself. Mostly. One out of every seven meals I cook is edible, but if a woman sticks around long enough, that one meal will knock her off her feet. I mention this because when I began looking for a life mate, I realized that my needs were mental, physical, and emotional. They had nothing to do with logistics.

I was once extremely attracted to a super-smart young lady who was into fitness, kind to other people, ambitious, and didn't need a man, but, for some reason, she was interested in me.

I have never been overly aggressive when it comes to affairs of the heart. I think, because of having been abandoned by my mother as a child, I am afraid of rejection. However, when I first began interacting with this woman, she made it clear that our interest was mutual and that gave me the nudge I needed to keep pursuing her. We had a good thing going in the beginning. We'd talk on the phone for hours and I'd plan romantic little dates. She struck me as fun and easygoing.

Then, approximately six months into the relationship, she began to question me about whom I was talking to on the phone, something she'd never done before. If I got off work later than expected, she accused me of making someone at work more important, even if I called to tell her I was running late. It got to the point that the relationship became a job in and of itself. It was beyond demanding. I had to text her good morning, give her a detailed list of what I was planning to do that day, and call if I had a break. When it came to going out with friends, I felt like a sixteen-year-old reporting to my mother. She had to know everyone I was going out with and what time I would be home. As much as I feared rejection, I feared being emasculated and losing my freedom even more. I quickly went from being eager and excited to see her to planning my exit strategy.

In the end, I broke up with my suddenly controlling girlfriend and considered it one more step in my journey toward the love I'd spend my life with.

On the quest for a happily-ever-after relationship, adding the right person into that space in your heart puts all of us romantic dreamers in a predicament. Like with life itself, everything worth having takes time.

Each one of us thinks we know what we are looking for and we continue to hold open interviews through our friends, dating sites, our social media pages, hoping the next one will be the right one. The gut feeling, we have during the courting process that, perhaps, the man or woman we've been spending time with has characteristics that make them Miss or Mr. Wrong is something we need to listen to, not wait to see if things will change.

Listen to your gut; it always knows. Men and women don't.

As with any trip you take in life, there are those places you fall madly in love with and you can't wait to get back to and do that thing all over again, and there are places you'll go that you promise never to return to. For most of us on the hero or she'ro journey, we need to be honest with that person who looks back at us in our mirrors. We can be in denial and need to see what is in front of us and know that what we see has been there from the very beginning—which is probably the reason you are reading this book or are out on a new date right now.

I recently trained a young lady for the first time and she asked me if I knew her friend "Bob the chiropractor" with whom she had recently broken up. She said he was still her best friend, but she was still trying to overcome the hurt from the breakup, even though "he was a great guy." (Hmmm.) She went on to tell me that she had been there with him through the tough times while he'd been going through school. But, she said, after graduating, their priorities headed in different directions; he into his new career and she toward her new life and being single.

When I hear a conversation like this, it hurts my heart. I wish I could save everyone from this kind of experience, but we have all been there. Because it's part of our life's journey, we continue to make reservations to take these kinds of emotional trips, looking for the hero's journey with that happy ending.

When you connect with the right person, their behavior should be stable, and if it is not, that might be a sign to cut bait and run. Each of us, when entering the hero's journey, starts so well. We are always there, open to offer help wherever and whenever we are needed. Before long, and I hear this all the time, you find yourself putting forth all the effort and getting little to nothing in return. You continue to try, hoping your partner will notice you are there for them. You hope when you are in need that their love and affection will be returned at the same level in which you are willing to give yours. But, in the end, you feel burned, used, get depressed, and blame yourself for being part of this relationship. You thought it was an all-expenses-paid trip, only to discover your emotional partner's account was overdrawn, and you are left to pay the bill. Emotionally, you find yourself working overtime to recover from the consequences of your actions. Why? Because our gut tells us we are falling into an emotional trap while our heart tells us to look for the good in others. We believe the next one will be and do differently. But you have been there and done that, so why continue acting and believing the same way?

Think about this: if we were to remove ourselves from where we are now and be honest and look back on all our relationships that ended badly, we would notice obvious short-comings and flaws with our partner in the early stages of the relationship. We prayed they would just go away. Please keep in mind, we have all been there, and it is okay. It is all part of our hero's journey.

I liken it to planning a trip. There are signs that tell you where and when to go or if you should risk it all and see what happens. For me, I can now tell within thirty minutes of conversation with a person if I want to spend or invest more time with them just by listening to them explain how they overcame or dealt with challenges in their past dating life or life in general. I also say *listen more than you talk*. The person will either open a door that will make you want to come back, or they will pull on the other side of the door, trying to prevent you from a speedy exit. People will show you who they are when things don't go as planned or in their treatment or feelings toward others.

Here is what I look out for when dealing with work or life issues. If your partner is in a bad mood and their entire day is shot, and everything you say or do to try to help make life better just makes things worse for your partner, and they take it out on you only to come back after the damage has been done to say they are sorry, this is a big warning sign. Between us, there is never a good reason to disrespect your partner when that partner is being respectful toward you. This would be a clear indication that this date/person may never grow into a relationship that would be part of your hero's journey.

Please do not get me wrong. With what is going on in the world we live in today, there are things out of our control, so understand that life will throw obstacles your way from time to time. We all have our problems to deal with and get upset over. But if your partner is a nightmare to be around when they feel challenged, this might be signs of a personality disorder and you may have to look at this person as a road not worth taking.

When things happen, I typically can just laugh them off and do my best not to get upset to the point where I am out of control. I seek direction from my well-respected friends to see if I was at fault or if they can suggest a better solution for how I should resolve whatever situation I am dealing with at that time. I went through this regarding visitations with my kids after my wife and I signed our divorce papers.

Because my kids were young, I didn't want them to experience what I went through when my parents split up. I tend to be a team player and I want everything to work just right for everyone. I still wanted to be part of "Team Family," but the relationship dynamic between my ex and I had changed. Because she was the mother of my children, I still felt the responsibility to make sure the kids' meals were on time as they'd been before the split, and when they were sick, I was there. Even when my ex got sick, I picked up things she needed and did little things for her without being asked. The way I was brought up taught me these were all actions of a person who'd promised to provide, protect, and care for the partner I'd brought into my life. Although it was no longer my responsibility to care and protect, I felt the need to show my children, through my actions, an example of how to treat a person who either loves you or you once loved.

Another thing I think you should strive for is being authentic, being the real you. In my everyday life, I say what I mean. I also do what I say. Sometimes when I speak my truth, I worry that I may have hurt the feelings of someone I care about. I respect openly honest people more so than those who tiptoe around how they really feel or what they really would like to say. Those types of people tiptoe because they are worried about hurting your feelings. Keep in mind when I say *be authentic;* I mean to be you, one hundred percent. Telling someone the truth is not being disrespectful; it is being honest. You should gravitate toward that kind of person when looking for a partner because you will always know they have no issues with telling you the truth.

When asked, "How do I look in this dress?" or "Is there something between your teeth?", your partner should have no reservations telling you that you are more beautiful in that red dress you wore in that picture in your living room over the very sexy black dress that plunges too far down the center of your chest and would not be appropriate for meeting your family for the first time. Or maybe it was okay to hang out at a sports bar when you first met but taking you there for a milestone birthday isn't the evening you envisioned.

If you want to see the perfect outline of a hero's journey, pick up a copy of Dr. Seuss' book *Oh, The Places You'll Go!* and envision the words on the pages as you are on your date. Going to all these places, you will discover the truth about your hero's journey, but, like the opening of this book, you have to be open and honest with the person sitting across from you right now. Remember this phrase while on this journey: *be authentic*.

CHAPTER EIGHTEEN

Chick Flicks

Anyone who knows me knows that I love movies. That means all movies—romantic comedies, dramas, action-adventure, sci-fi, horror, documentaries, westerns, and even (believe it or not) Disney/Pixar flicks. My kids all claim to be too old to see family-friendly PG and animated movies with me, so I see them alone.

I'm the first one to own that I have yet to grow up and movies provide a healthy outlet for my dreamer's mind. I find them a welcome escape from life's pressures and stressors.

When I was first dating my ex-wife, I proposed a movie-watching pact. If she'd agree to see a movie I was interested in and she didn't enjoy it, she would get to pick the next two movies with no input or objection from me.

The first movie she picked was *Pretty Woman*. Until then, as a staunchly heterosexual male with some—at the time common, but now outdated and abandoned—ideas about what was expected from someone of my gender, I was silently kicking and screaming all the way to the theater. Today, Julia Roberts is one of my favorite actresses and I've seen almost every one of her films. But, at that time, I wasn't expecting to like the movie, yet I wanted to connect with my partner. I was, and am, a person of my word.

The weekend came and went, and when I got to work, I told one of my then clients at the sports training institute in New York, Richard LaGravenese, whom I did not know was in the movie industry, that I had spent an hour and a half watching a chick flick. As Richard sat on the bench waiting for me to set up his next exercise, he began to chuckle to himself.

"What did you think of the movie?" he asked.

"I loved it!" I gushed. I then proceeded to go on and on about the characters and to give a play-by-play recap of my favorite scene when Richard Gere's character took Julia Roberts' character shopping.

"We're going to spend an obscene amount of money, so we'll need an obscene amount of sucking up." From the movie Pretty Woman "Love this movie."

After I'd finished my rave review and he'd finished his next set, Richard told me he was one of the staff writers for Touchstone at that time and had worked on the project. It was then that I told him I aspired to become a screenwriter someday. Everyone has a dream, and this was only one of many.

Much to my excitement and mortification, Richard asked if he could see my work. I was apprehensive. I was an amateur and he was a professional. I figured I couldn't say no though, given that he trusted me to help him reach his physical goals, I thought I owed it to myself to trust him with my career aspirations.

The two weeks it took Richard to read my screenplay were the longest two weeks of my life.

After he had reviewed my work, his feedback floored me.

"Kevin," he said. "You are the worst screenwriter I have ever met."

I felt as if he'd delivered a cruel sucker punch. My knees were wobbly, and I wanted to take to my bed and sob like a baby. The idea that I wasn't very good had occurred to me. But worse, the demoralization was complete. It was also short-lived.

Richard continued. He said he knew a lot of screenwriters in Hollywood who were making good livings in the film industry and that I was better than at least half of them. He said I was one of the best storytellers he knew, and he encouraged me to keep writing and then to find people who could help me with craft, formatting, and technique.

I credit Richard for providing the inspiration for me to keep going as a writer. Whenever I start to lose hope or momentum, I think about his words and I keep writing.

Each of us has deep-seated passions and desires. There are things we want to do and things that light us up inside that make us interesting and special. Unfortunately, fear can be an impediment to self-expression. Whether you're reluctant to sit in a theater and watch a chick-flick or are hesitant to show a rough draft of your screenplay to a trusted acquaintance, or anything else you both do and don't want to do, I say pursue your dreams. If you're wondering how these fit into the subject of dating, I'm of the opinion that the more well-rounded you are as an individual, the more you can contribute to being a couple.

To get beyond the first date and into a relationship, you must have interests to talk about, values in common, and experiences to share. Let your date in on your dreams, but, even better, let them be part of your path to turning those dreams into reality.

Although I still love chick flicks, I've learned not to base real-life romance on what we see depicted on the screen. Healthy relationships have a minimum of drama, encourage authentic self-expression, and don't require either person to change for the other while inspiring both to evolve together.

I believe that movies allow us to escape life, but we can't base our relationship ideals on what the movies tell us about love. Let's use *Pretty Woman* as an example. The movie is the story of a down-on-her-luck prostitute who, after being rescued by a wealthy businessman, transforms herself and, as a result, finds love in the end. The idealist in me imagines happily-ever-after, but the realist understands an overly ambitious workaholic and an undereducated woman from the wrong side of the tracks likely have little in common. When looking for lasting love, let it be okay to find something enduring, compatible, and full of depth with little drama.

In most of the books I have written to date, you will find one of my many taglines. They are the following.

Love like it's your last day on earth Yesterday is history. No matter how hard we try, whatever we did yesterday, no one can change it; it is whatever it is.

Laugh like it's how you make your living. There is no successful comedian living the dream life who is not funny. What I am saying is to enjoy each day of your life and be fulfilled not in your life, but in the lives of those you have touched. Always leave them with a smile.

Love like you're writing your own story. When your life comes to an end, which we all will face someday, will it be a Dramedy, an Action-Adventure, Sci-fi, Comedy, Horror, Porn, Documentary, or the greatest love story ever told?

Just for fun, take a pen to paper and write a synopsis of what your story would be. To be fair, I will share with you the synopsis I wrote for the screenplay I allowed Richard to read.

Please keep in mind, the screenplay today is much better than the one Richard read. One day, three of my books and this screenplay will be featured either on the big screen or on Netflix.

****

THE DEAL

an original screenplay
by
Kevin McLemore

A struggling white screenwriter devises a plan to break into show business by having his African American neighbors' teenage son pretend to have written one of his screenplays.

James Anthony is a thirty-five-year-old wannabe screenwriter living in the suburban house he grew up in. After his father's untimely death, James begrudgingly takes over the struggling family business selling insurance door-to-door, and, in one fell swoop, finds himself working a job he hates and being saddled with a crippling mortgage, not to mention the growing piles of rejection letters from agents on both coasts who see no profit in a part-time writer living in Cleveland with no credits or connections.

Then, one day, the Neils, an African American family, move into the house next door. James becomes friendly with their son, Raymond, and devises an audacious plan to get Hollywood interested in one of his screenplays: Raymond will pretend he wrote the script. James will act as Raymond's manager, and agents and movie studios alike will be so impressed, they'll be tripping over one another to get at the seventeen-year-old screenwriting prodigy.

At the same time, Robin, James' first love who disappeared after their magical summer together over twenty years ago, reappears on the scene and James sets out to win her heart all over again. This works like a charm... with only one small wrinkle. Even though Robin makes it very clear that she believes in telling the truth at all costs, James decides not to tell her about his half-baked idea to make it big in the movie business.

Meanwhile, James' Hollywood scheme ends up working like a charm as well, and soon, he and Raymond are on their way to Los Angeles to meet with some of the film world's best and brightest. The only problem with the plan is that Raymond is a little too good at playing the part of the whiz kid screenwriter and James finds himself getting jealous of all the attention Ray's getting...

Surrounded by a motley crew of well-meaning friends, disapproving parents, nosy neighbors, double-dealing agents, Tinseltown bigwigs, and a puppy named Happy, James somehow manages to not only untangle his web of lies, find the success he so richly deserves, and get the girl of his dreams, but he also learns a few life lessons along the way.

CHAPTER NINETEEN

This Is My Baby, And You Are...?

I am not sure when this started, but there is a trend going on.

It may have come with those late-night commercials for ASPCA featuring abandoned or abused animals, but people who once had a single dog took on a partner with a child and cats, and now have a family, dogs, cats and a child.

There is no surprise with the rising divorce rate there are partners without a partner who have children at home. So, if I can trend, single-parent dating is on the rise, and pet-minded moms and dads are searching for their human soulmates, to either fill or replace the other soulmate they thought they had the first time around.

However, the toughest part of a conversation with someone is the truth about just how much baggage they carry around with them when being either introduced or inserted into another person's life. They say timing is everything, but does that apply to a first date? If no, why? If yes, why?

Throughout my research for this book, one of the major issues people had was when was the right time to disclose just how much your partner-to-be was still connected to their children, their ex-partner, their pets, and if they'd sworn off ever dating again or were now open to only dating partners of the same sex.

With all the experts and rules surrounding the conversation of how to find true love or your soulmate, we overlook the deal breaker or avoid the conversation on our first couple of dates. Wait, I'll let you think.

Okay, let me help. If you had to pick one conversation, would it be about your pets, your child or children, the race or sexual orientation of your child, your friendship with your ex? Are you following me now?

Common sense says *all of the above*, but pets' relationship with their owner and dating became a noted issue when talking to couples about relationships for this book. I thought it would be children, but I learned a lot about just how close some people were to their pets and the cause and effect that relationship had on their current and past relationships; it was a deal breaker going forward in the dating world.

To me, the way a person treats their pets speaks to how they'll treat you and where you may fall in the pecking order when it comes to his or her needs. The same goes for children. Well-laid plans with partners with kids and pets are always subject to change. People who have had bad experiences with past instant-family relationships or who have never had a relationship with a cat- or a dog-lover, may find themselves in a battle where the children and/or the pets win.

Both men and women struggle with the timing as to when to bring up the conversation of their children. Their reason is fear.

It is human nature to avoid situations or conversations that will turn a good time into a bad time. While at the time, we put off the conversation that needs to be had for the *right* time, and avoid the *right* time for a *good* time. We wait for that right time (which is now) to talk about something you should have had the first time it popped into your head. Which is the reason there are 54 cards in this book to help if you have any issues knowing when it is the right time.

Let me help you with this example. When is it a good time to tell your new partner/date that the other side of your pillow is never cool, because it is always occupied by 120-pound friend name Buddy?

Do you mention them on date one? Or do you wait until the first sleepover to let your date know that the side of the bed, they're now occupying is typically occupied by Buddy, your 120 lb. German Shepherd Dog or your three-year-old, neither of whom are happy to be locked out of the room?

You must understand and respect the connection your potential partner has with their children and/or pet(s).

There's no one right or wrong answer as to when you should let your date know the actual size of your family or how long before you want to bring them around to meet your pet or your children. Personally, however, I think you should aim to disclose these things before there is an emotional connection with the person sitting across from you.

Introducing your date to your children and your pet as early as possible will help you figure out the potential for longevity. When it comes to an emotional connection or commitment with a man or woman with either pets or beloved children already in their life, your plus one must be authentic to what he or she is ready to deal and live with long-term.

If your date is not a pet lover, if they care for you, they will become one. If they're not crazy about children, if they see a future with you, they'll make a special exception and become fast friends with you and yours. This is so important, especially if your pet is part of the bull breed or your children are biracial.

If your date has kids, you need to get to know them sooner rather than later; you don't want to be emotionally attached to someone who will create an emotional divide between you and your children or who doesn't have a strong attachment to his or her own family.

My advice is to make the introduction early. This doesn't necessarily mean on the first few dates, but certainly before you have given them too much of yourself.

The other option would be to ask for advice from someone you respect and trust, like my oldest daughter did this morning while I was on my way to work. It was around 10:35 a.m. when the phone in my car rang.

"Hello, sweetheart," I said.

This call was not our normal time to talk. Our call times are normally Thursdays after work or Saturday evenings, and usually on my drive home from work. Figuring something was wrong, I asked, "What's going on?"

She responded, "Why nothing. Can't I just call?"

"Sure," I said, but when I get an unscheduled call in the daytime from my children, it's normally bad news or a request to send money. In this instance, it was neither.

My daughter wanted to let me know she was going out on a date. Funny, she's forty-two years old. Why would she call me to tell me about a pending date? Was she pregnant? Was she dating someone I needed to make "disappear"? I had no idea why I was on this call, so I asked. "Why are you telling me this?" I pulled over to brace myself. I didn't want to overreact but prepared myself in case I had to go to Atlanta and act a fool.

She asked if I knew T.O. Who? T.O.? I only knew one person who could not spell his own name and he was a professional football player. I could not envision my daughter with Terrell Owens. This could not be the same man.

Oh, was I oh-so-wrong!

Hell no, I thought. Then I caught myself. I was overreacting and I had to calm myself down. I had to speak from my heart and not from the airline ticket I was about to buy while only checking in a baseball bat as my carry-on. All kidding aside, I asked, "Do you know who this man is, and do you know his story?" She declined to google her date which I suggested she do right away. By the way, I had gotten upset when I'd found out my ex had googled me before we'd gone out, but this is my daughter, not me. This was "The" Terrell Owens with multiple baby mommas. I did not want my little girl added to his list of women he had loved and left with a parting gift. He wasn't going to stay around long enough to learn the correct spelling of his full name.

Now, please understand, I overreacted to this news. My daughter is old enough to make her own mistakes. But this is the kind of guy who needs to be authentic from "Hello." Why? Because It's the right thing to do. Even if he has changed, this is a conversation my daughter needs to hear from him first, not google.

She doesn't need to hear or to be featured on the cover of one of those magazines you see in the grocery store featuring the worst parts of his celebrity life.

I do trust my oldest daughter's judgment. But I still wanted to talk to this man before he put his car into park in my daughter's driveway. He needs to know that fathers still know best, and he needs to be on point when it comes to my daughter. It is not my position to pick or choose whom my children date. In this case, however, I believe he should reveal his intention to her as soon as possible. She should understand who this man is and confirm early on if he is a different man than he was before. I am sure my ex would say the same about me if asked.

The nice thing about this share, no one needs to ask me if she ever went out with him or dated him. All I need to say is that I am happy that my daughter is smarter than that.

So be it your pet or your children, your date needs to know, upfront, your position as to the total package you bring into this relationship. Flip the next card.

CHAPTER TWENTY

Passion

When you think about passion as it relates to dating, you probably think about the I-want-to-rip-your-clothes-off feeling that some might label lust and others will refer to as chemistry. Don't get me wrong, I'm all for that kind of passion. Every intimate relationship should contain moments of physical magnetism. The more moments, the better. But if you want sustained attraction to another person and if you want to be attractive in a way that lasts, your passion must expand beyond the boundaries of the bedroom.

There is something magical about being around a person who is lit up about something. Have you ever spoken to someone about their work or hobbies and watched them come alive before your very eyes as they describe the thing they find most compelling? That kind of excitement isn't just contagious, it's sexy.

The things that are most important to you, that drive and inspire you, make you the most vibrant and authentic version of yourself and it's that version of you that is the most alluring to others. This is one of the great dating paradoxes and an essential thing to pay attention to. I've known a lot of people, men, and women, who've been incredibly passionate about certain causes or activities only to meet someone, get into a relationship, then give up the things they used to do, only to wonder why the spark has faded.

A person's passion flows from them like a river from a source. The minute they stop pursuing what excites them is the minute they grow stagnant. A lot of the most successful couples are successful because both partners find a shared passion, but having overlapping interests isn't essential. What *is* essential is that you find someone who encourages you to be excited by life and for whom you do the same.

Whenever someone comes to me for life coaching or professional personal training, I make it my mission to link behaviors to emotions. This is because I know the likelihood of them taking consistent actions over time greatly increases if they are passionate about the process and not just the results. A few years ago, I worked with two different clients, both male, both around the same age, and both with the same weight loss goals. As I talked to the first man about how we were going to get him to lose the thirty pounds he needed to lose, he told me about how much he values his connections to friends and family and how little he likes spending his free time alone. I knew immediately what to do! I had this client enroll in a men's basketball league, sign up for a block of yoga sessions with his wife, and agree to take his kids out each weekend to practice their soccer skills and kick the ball around.

When the second client came to see me, he spoke about his love of learning and his desire to one day become a well-known podcaster. I asked him to make me one simple promise. "Until you reach your weight loss goal, will you commit to only listening to podcasts while engaged in some form of fitness?" He thought the recommendation was strange, but because he listened to at least four podcasts a week and looked forward to the release of every new episode, he'd just agreed to be in the gym or out on the road, running, walking, or biking, at least four days out of the week.

Within three months, my second client was three pounds away from his goal. We both agreed he looked great and shifted our plan to maintenance. Within five months, client number one exceeded his goal by seven pounds and was wearing clothes he hadn't fit into since college (only around the house of course, considering they'd long since gone out of fashion).

With over thirty-five years of helping people create the lasting changes they say they want; I've learned that passion generates momentum and that the *lack* of passion makes forward movement halting and unlikely. The same is true in our romantic relationships. When dating, look for a potential partner whose passions you can support, and/or become involved in, and who will do the same for you.

What you desire, what brings you the most pleasure, what you are truly passionate about... these are all important questions to ask in dating and in life.

You never gain anything in life by being lackadaisical about the things you strongly believe in. You gain even less by denying your true values. On your next date, ask the person you're with, "What are you most passionate about? What lights you up? What inspires you?" or any variation of the same. And, in the meantime, ask these questions of yourself. The more you cultivate passion in life, the more likely you'll be to find it in love, but you first must discover your *why*.

There is a science behind the conversations you have in your head and the words that motivate, engage, and influence your life. When your heart is into something or someone, the passion of your *why* can move mountains. What we are most driven by are words and actions that shape our thoughts, our feelings, and directly reflect our emotional input and output when it comes to the matter of the heart.

When two people connect, there is a never-ending emotional negotiation between two people trying to motivate the other to see life their way, or sacrificing their needs for their partner, and hoping that at some point their needs will be addressed.

However, a relationship in many ways is like interviewing for a job and getting it, only later realizing that you're begging, bribing, threatening, and reasoning them to death. Put just as much interest into maintaining what drew the two of you together so that you don't find yourself so desperate that you start nagging, manipulating or deceiving to get your way.

Dating With A Full Deck starts with an understanding that both parties enter the date with a low expectation of a long-term relationship but a commitment to be one hundred percent honest with the person you are now on a date with, without judgement or perceived prejudices from past relationships. This, in my world, is getting to the first *yes*. The only goal here is to communicate honestly. The deck of cards associated with this book makes it easy for each of you to follow through and do what you both promised to do when agreeing to go out together.

Understanding a person's passion is not about understanding their goals; it is understanding where they place their values and if they are finishers or starters. Going out on a first date is a small goal; getting that person to see you again is next in the process.

Hours before I started to edit this chapter, I sat with two female friends who were both looking for a good man, and when I explained that there was no such thing as a good man, that all men were dogs—

including Yours Truly—they were shocked. However, I went on to say that a man must have a good reason to go against his natural urge to hunt and conquer, and find a good reason to change his natural behavior.

When I asked the one young lady—let's call her Heather—why she hadn't been successful in her last relationship, she said he'd lied about everything. Before I gave her my two cents and asked what issues she'd had with the last three men she'd dated, she said her previous boyfriends had lied, too.

I wanted to know what her dates lied about. The list was small, like what time he was coming over, not giving full details as to which friends he was out with, and a couple of other little things that bothered her. When I asked her how she'd reacted to his lies, she said that, because of her past relationships, she went off on him.

Not surprised by her answer, I was more surprised by her response to my next question. This is the same question I would ask a guy when it comes to the conversation of failed relationships. "What was your relationship with your father, and what was your mother like?"

Why did I ask this question? It's because of reasons outside my pay grade. Both men and women have, on different levels, indirectly—and some directly—mastered the art of manipulation. I am not one hundred percent sure we can blame everything as adults on mommy and daddy issues, but we are going into a new relationship open and flexible. As the relationship develops, we start to see little things we think we need to change about the person we are with—like needing to know where the person is every second of the day, having dinner ready at a certain time or not being willing to go out on the weekends like you did when you'd first started to date.

If your relationship starts over the top in the romance department and it begins to decline later on in the relationship because life starts to get in the way and your partner is over the top still, and now the conversation about your sex life turns from a welcome conversation to a very uncomfortable daily topic, one or both will try to manipulate the other to get their way. If you've had children and tried to get them to do something they don't want to do, the same thing will happen with this conversation—nothing and the protest will begin.

There are so many layers as to why some relationships flourish while others flounder. Some men and women are true manipulators. They create a situation that sets up a good relationship to fail just because they have not taken enough interest in reprogramming what they'd learned from either past relationships or their own narcissistic behavior.

Stop! Before your read on, note this.

Dating With A Full Deck is designed to just have fun while out on a first date, and let me emphasize *fun* so that you are having such a good time, that you'll want to see this person again.

If there are signs early in the dating process that resemble patterns of past failed relationships, you'll want to reexamine the entire relationship. It doesn't matter how physically attractive the person is or how successful they are or how great the sex was in the beginning; if the patterns are there, you know the outcome.

We are *solely* responsible for the expectation of the relationship. We are *solely* responsible how we react to when the expectation is no longer being met. We must understand that, if our date starts out being open and honest at the beginning but you later—because of past experiences—start to question that honesty, you are also *solely* responsible for *not* putting that person in a position where it's easier for them to "bend the truth" than to deal with how you will react to their dishonesty.

If you know anyone who has ever tried to change a person's behavior, through motivation or manipulation, you know that they failed. If that person is you, then you understand *why* you are still single and looking for the right person.

Passion, on so many levels, is an extremely strong and controllable emotion that can be applied to art, work, travel, sex, life, social activism, the environment, and even dating and relationships.

To understand your passion, start with your *why*.

CHAPTER TWENTY-ONE
Confidence

It's sad and startling to think about just how many people struggle with issues of self-esteem. I would be remiss if I didn't talk about this because nowhere are our insecurities more obvious than in the realm of dating. An unregulated sense of self can be one of our biggest barriers to creating healthy relationships with others, but, even more destructively, poor self-esteem negatively impacts our most important (and only inescapable) relationship: the one we have with ourselves.

A lot of people mean different things when they talk about self-esteem, and because it is a term that is often used, I consider it essential to explain what I mean when I talk about the subject.

The dictionary defines self-esteem as *confidence in one's own worth or abilities, self-respect.* I think it can be dangerous to tie our self-respect to our abilities as opposed to our actions. When working with a new client, I tell them that self-esteem builds the more we take actions that take us in the direction of our vision and our values.

The strongest among us aren't strong because they don't have any shortcomings. They're strong because they've accurately assessed themselves, know their weaknesses, and own their strengths. Confidence does not equal arrogance, and feelings of inferiority have no place in the realm of dating.

Imagine the following dating scenarios: a young woman who thinks she can do nothing right and struggles with shame and self-hatred goes out with a kind and generous man who is initially very interested in her. They sit across the table. Over appetizers, she complains about the circumference of her thighs, talks about how uneducated she is because she never finished college, and how she lacks the skills to acquire better than an entry-level job. When the main meal arrives, he asks her about her interests, and she says, "Oh I don't know, I'm a pretty boring person." By dessert, is it any wonder that he's looking for the exit? This woman has zero self-esteem, and her lack of self-love would drive anyone of substance away.

Let's take a woman with the same set of circumstances and send her on a date. Secretly suffering from the same insecurities but overcompensating with arrogance, she talks about how envious all her girlfriends are of her curves, how she's so brilliant she didn't need a degree, and how she's so awesome to be around that she's not a "joiner." By the end of the evening, her date is also looking to escape. So, what might healthy self-esteem look like?

A young woman goes on a date with a man, sits across from him, and happily orders the evening's specials. "I love a good meal," she says with a smile. "How about you? Are you a foodie, too?" She and her date talk about their favorite cuisines and connect over their love of decadent treats and their need to compensate with trips to the gym. When he asks about her education, she tells him, without flinching, that she left school to care for a sick parent and never went back, thereby earning his esteem as a person who values family and responsibility. "I do think of going back someday," she says, voicing a dream and creating an opportunity for connection. "I love to learn, and a degree would open up some doors for me." He admires her ambition and sees her as the imperfect yet evolving person that she is. When he asks about hobbies, she says, "I'm looking for more fun ways to spend my time. Any suggestions?" See how much more engaging this woman is?

No matter who we are or where we are in life, we deserve love. We also deserve to own our authentic values and experiences. Rather than attempting to impress your date with how incredible you are, or to evoke their pity by playing the martyr, own your victories and your mistakes in a way that makes it clear you're not looking for someone to complete you because you're complete within yourself. Complete doesn't mean cocky and it doesn't mean you don't need anyone else. It means you know your worth and you're looking to connect with someone from a place of giving and receiving.

There is nothing wrong with owning your successes, provided you can also acknowledge your failures. Accurate and unapologetic self-assessment is critical to giving someone the information they need to get to know you—and vice versa. How would you feel if you went on a date with someone who told you they rarely drink and go to heavy metal shows "every once in a while," only to discover after a few months that they have a nightly beer, get sloshed every weekend, and go to concerts three nights a month? Sometimes, on dates, people tell each other what they *think* the other person wants to hear when they should be telling the truth to assess their compatibility. The beer-loving music fan would be much happier with another music aficionado with a taste for Sam Adams than a teetotaler who doesn't know the difference between Dave Matthews and David Bowie.

When I moved from Cleveland, Ohio to New York City to pursue a career as an actor, I quickly realized that I wasn't about to be the next blockbuster star, considering I had no training, no connections, no agent, and no clue. Luckily, I landed a job at the then New York Sports Institute, where I worked alongside fifteen of New York's best professional trainers. The club's list of clients reads like a Who's Who of movers and shakers. I had the chance to train some of the most prominent influencers in the entertainment industry, wealthy Wall Street businesspeople, and even the late Mayor of New York, Ed Koch.

In my first year, I was voted one of the top professional trainers by *Inc. Magazine.* As prestigious as this award was, I was humbled. Like all the other trainers I worked with and learned from, all of whom I had considered better at the job than me, I believed (and still believe) that the client is the real superstar. My role as a trainer has always been to reach another person and motivate them to see the diamond in themselves. For most of my female clients, I teach—or remind them—that the first person they need to learn to love is themselves.

I have come to see, in retrospect, that what separated me from any of the other deserving trainers who did not make *Inc. Magazine*'s list was that I never looked at my profession as a job or even a career. I looked at it as a craft and a calling. My *why.* I put my heart and soul into meeting the needs of my clients because being a trainer has always felt like more than what I do; it is who I am.

In the realm of relationships, it can take a lot of courage to walk up to a person and ask them for a date, but the capacity to do that will be increased if you know that all human beings are valuable and deserve to get their needs met.

There will always be those people who will criticize or condemn you for your personal beliefs and/or for how you see yourself, but that will be true no matter where you are in life. It is impossible to please everybody. At the end of the day, the best we can do is to surround ourselves with people with whom we can be authentic. While no other person on this earth can complete you, you want to find people that complement you by adding to your life and valuing all of you—the good, the bad, and the ugly.

The most baffling thing about self-confidence is that it is not necessarily tied to any verifiable truths. Some people look in the mirror and suffer from dysmorphia, seeing their bodies reflected in ways that are not accurate. Anorexics starve themselves and still perceive their bodies as "fat." People who become addicted to plastic surgery see every minor bump and blemish in need of intervention. Although this sort of extreme misperception is not common, many human beings suffer from forms of distorted self-appraisal. *Dating With A Full Deck* is an invitation to be rigorously honest—first with yourself, then with your date.

If you find that you have trouble knowing your true value, ask yourself this question: *If I were my own best friend, what would I say about myself?*

We tend to see our friends accurately. We know their strengths and weaknesses and we love them as they are. So do the same for yourself and you will begin to evaluate yourself with greater accuracy, an invaluable life skill that will carry over, not only into dating, but into every aspect of your life.

I must add jealousy and connect it with how both men and women put themselves out there. I have been in dating situations where the person I thought I was dating would openly flirt with other guys to create a reaction, to get me to fight for her affection and not run the risk of losing her. This strategy has never worked for me, and I am sure for many like me, this juvenile behavior did not strengthen their relationships either.

It has backfired on every woman who has ever tried it. Now, for some men and women this tactic, i.e., "flirting with someone," while you are in earshot of the conversation, taking a drink from a stranger while on a date with you, spending time with a female friend who has openly proclaimed that if your date ever became free, they would love to go out with them, has worked. There are a lot of reasons people deploy this jealousy strategy. Some use it to keep the dates attached to them and others use this abusive behavior strategy to control.

I know, for me, I deployed this strategy when I discovered the person I had given my heart and soul to had cheated on me. As much as I wanted to be true, I had put myself out there like the betrayal hadn't bothered me. But it had. It'd crushed me. I told her that we could still be friends. When she asked if I was seeing anyone, I confirmed there was someone I had an interest in and about all the great conversations I'd had with this person who did not exist. My confidence when it came to women was at such a low level, my only strategy was to listen to my own words, and work on rebuilding my head and my heart.

One would be surprised by the triggers in life that will either build you up or break you down, but it is almost impossible to attract something good in your life if you have something smelly on your hook.

CHAPTER TWENTY-TWO

The End... And The Beginning

Although it's a commonly stated social truism that nearly fifty percent of all marriages end in divorce, statistics estimate that the rate is closer to forty or forty-five percent. I never imagined *I* would fall within that group. I'd expected my marriage to last forever. What I hadn't anticipated was that when two flawed human beings fall for each other, love is not enough. They must communicate, agree, and build.

Relationships are a negotiation between "I" and "we."

I like to say, "Before you, there was me." What I mean by this is that, prior to embarking on a romantic partnership, each person has their own life experiences. Having insight into another person's history, where they are from, what they want out of life, what subjects interest them, their religious beliefs, their political affiliations, sexual interest or non-interest, sports, foods, fitness, etc. are essential to know if you'll be compatible with them.

A person's history is a clear indication of what they have learned in life, how they've evolved, their patterns, their choices, and their character. That's not to say people who've made mistakes are destined to repeat them, but, when talking to someone in whom you're interested, how they speak about their past is a good indicator of whether they've learned from their failures. For instance, if someone's been divorced, ask them what went wrong in their marriage then listen to see if their explanation offers any insights. People who refuse to be accountable for their pasts are destined for dysfunctional futures.

A person who has no connection with their history has no chance of lasting happiness. This doesn't mean wallowing. Far from it!

It wasn't until I took responsibility for my part in the dissolution of my marriage that I could fully open myself to finding love again. That didn't mean it was effortless or that I didn't suffer setbacks along the way.

Learning to move through life with grace, dignity, and self-respect is a lot like learning any other skill. When you were a baby first learning to walk, you fell a lot as you figured out how to balance. Then there was the period of instability as you moved from someone who could walk, haltingly, to being steady on your feet. Eventually, you were able to run full-speed ahead and your initial unsteadiness was nothing more than a distant memory.

When my kids were growing up, they each took very different approaches to learning how to walk. But, in the end, no matter their approach, all that was required was for them to keep getting up after every fall. Life is the same. We fall, we get up, we make modifications, and we move forward in the direction we want to go.

If you go out on a date with someone and notice that they seem unable or unwilling to get up, dust themselves off, change their approach, and continue, you'd do well to run (not walk) in the opposite direction.

The only person standing between you and a healthy, happy relationship is *you*. If you haven't found what you're looking for, think about how you've been approaching dating and be willing to adapt your approach to achieve better results.

Being raised by my father's parents, I'd had a first-row seat to the kind of relationship I wanted for myself and my loved ones. When the time came to enter adulthood and take control of my life, I'd promised myself I would maintain the values they'd instilled in me. Ultimately, I was only partially successful. My first wife and I were great parents, but we weren't especially good partners.

I have come to believe that the failure of my marriage doesn't mean that I failed as a person. There's no shame in being among those who've moved through a divorce. But there is responsibility. I grew up with a dark cloud over my head because my parents split up. I internalized the pain of their failed marriage and, throughout my early life, anytime anyone asked about my parents, I avoided their questions and evaded any in-depth conversations.

I carried the beliefs of childhood into adulthood and, when my marriage unraveled, I initially went into a downward spiral. It turned out, however, that the end of my marriage was the beginning of healing the unresolved wounds of my past. I did a lot of soul-searching in the aftermath of my divorce. I thought about where I hadn't been happy, where I hadn't contributed to my ex's happiness, and what I'd learned about communication and commitment.

It's important to know that, in the early days of dating, some people are comfortable disclosing everything and anything, whereas others would rather peel back the layers of disclosure slowly over time. There is no right way to open up to one another but being open is essential. Let yourself share authentically and invite your potential partner to do the same.

Interest increases along with authenticity. If a date is going well, you'll notice that you'll want to share yourself with the other person, and vice versa. If you want stimulation beyond your original physical attraction, then it would be wise to reveal yourself from the beginning. It's okay to disclose in stages. In fact, it's advisable. Rest assured that, if you begin with an open dialogue and set a precedent for sharing and connection, in time, you will find out everything you need to know about one another and be willing to make emotional and behavioral adjustments without sacrificing any aspects of yourself.

Let things flow naturally but be sure they're flowing forward. Lastly, note that neither you nor your date are the same person today as you were yesterday.

CHAPTER TWENTY-THREE

Do-Overs

One of my all-time favorite movies is *Groundhog Day*, starring Bill Murray. The movie premise is simple. An overzealous news reporter who has been demoted is assigned to cover a news story he believes to be beneath him. The news reporter starts as a pompous and entitled jerk. Then, through some strange twist in time, he finds himself doomed to repeat the same day (day after day) until he gets it right and evolves into a gentle soul and all-around good guy. In the end, he gets the girl, but only after he's admitted his shortcomings to himself and others.

We have all made our fair share of mistakes and done things we wouldn't have if we'd known then what we know now, but because life doesn't offer any do-overs, all we have is the opportunity to learn, evolve, and take every opportunity to be a better version of ourselves.

My list of things I'd do differently, if given a second chance, is long.

When it comes to dating, one of my biggest mistakes was canceling my senior prom date with a family friend, Robin, at the last minute. In hindsight, my reasoning was stupid and tied to my need to impress others, and my willingness to abandon my wants and needs to do so. My grandmother was partial to another girl, Linda, and thought—knowing what I now know—I should have gone with her instead.

If I could go back in time, I'd have picked Robin up in a limo and given her the best corsage I could afford with my very limited funds. I'm not saying I think Robin was "the one that got away" or anything of the sort, but I've come to value personal integrity in a way I wasn't capable of in high school. At that time, I was selfish and too dumb to be aware of it. Asking her to go to prom with me then rescinding my invitation so I could go out with Linda was wrong on all kinds of levels. I was shallow and spineless for not going with my gut and staying true to my initial invite. To this day, it is still one of those decisions I wish I could have reversed. My high school prom was hell night. I say that, in life with two options—Chance or Choice—it's your actions that define both.

Years have passed. I've grown up and am a much better person now than then. I hope Robin has forgotten all about me or forgiven me in a way. Unfortunately, I'll never know because she has (quite rightly) refused to speak to me ever since I let her down by not taking her to prom. Maybe one day our paths will cross, and I can ask for forgiveness, but would understand the position she would take. I made a horrible choice that day, and will live out my days, regretting the chance I took.

Life is no *Groundhog Day*. We don't get to replay the same events with the same people who conveniently forget every mistake we've made while we work out where we went wrong and win them over in the end. Life will, however, grow and stretch our character so we become better versions of ourselves, either for the same people or for different ones.

My guess is that I'm not the only person in this world who wishes they had the magic power to go back in time and do things over whenever we don't get them right the first time around.

Maybe you've let someone walk out of your life only to later realize they were great. Maybe you cheated on a partner and immediately recognized it was a mistake. Maybe you didn't ask a person out and regretted it. There are innumerable ways we fail to live up to our goals and our values. That's a huge part of being human. At one point or another, everyone craves a fresh start, and reentering the dating world is an opportunity to get it right, but only if we commit to refusing to repeat the same familiar wrongs.

It's likely that, if you've had multiple relationships in the past, there are patterns that you've carried forward from one to another. When you embark on a new relationship, you owe it to yourself to do things differently.

We've all made choices we wish we hadn't—or *not* made choices we wish we had—but there's no use regretting it if these things can't be changed. If you've hurt someone and can rectify the damage in some way without hurting them or yourself, I'd encourage you to do that. But if it's not possible, and even if it is, it's essential that we internalize the lessons of our past.

We are not doomed to recreate the same problems or live out the repetitive negative patterns of our past. Our mistakes teach us invaluable life lessons that allow us to become the heroes of our life journeys.

The key to any successful relationship is the willingness to improve. If you're fortunate enough to meet someone with whom you intend to spend a long-lasting relationship, you need to be willing to make incremental alterations over time. So, as you move forward with someone new, carry the best parts of your past forward. And if you're struggling to determine what the best parts are, think about the lessons you've gleaned, the improvements in your character, the positive memories, and the love you've internalized and retained. All these things will serve you well and often as you find your happily-ever-after person.

CHAPTER TWENTY-FOUR
Love Yourself, Love Someone Else

If you want to be in a lasting relationship with somebody else, first develop a relationship with yourself. Although this book is a book about dating, the most successful daters are those who embrace being single. This might seem counterintuitive, but it's true.

Being single for a while, especially after a failed relationship, is one of the best gifts you can give yourself. The single life offers an opportunity for introspection, personal development, and discovery.

You can choose to have new experiences, date interesting people, explore the world, and figure out what you're prepared to give to a potential partner.

My dad always said, "You will never miss what you never had, but you also never forget all the fun you used to have before you gave it up for what you have right now."

I've met many married people who got together young and didn't get to know themselves independently before committing themselves to someone else. Some of these people have confessed to me that they feel unfulfilled. On the other hand, I have met many single people who talk about being lonely and wanting a relationship. I don't think any of these people's discontentment is proof of the adage about the grass always being greener. I think it speaks to the fact that we want to know both what we're gaining and what we're giving up.

If you let yourself embrace being single and all it has to offer, you'll be far more equipped to embrace a relationship with a potential partner.

I always advise my coaching clients—those in and out of relationships—to "date" themselves. This means taking themselves on actual planned and intentional solo dates, something that can be incredibly enlightening. When I first instituted this practice, I discovered all sorts of things I didn't know about myself. For example, I prefer casual restaurants to fancy ones, activity-based dates, and doing things outdoors. I started planning fun things to do along the way. I might plan for a date with someone else. I asked myself the questions, "What would I love to do? What would make me happy? What new things do I want to try?" Those of my clients who were brave enough to go to dinner and a movie alone, or go to a museum unaccompanied, or anything else that sounded fun to them, learned a lot about themselves and cultivated a better relationship with the person they saw every morning in the mirror. They opened their eyes to their relationship with themselves and discovered what was lacking—and what was going well. One of my clients started getting dressed up for herself, wearing sexy lingerie when she knew only she would see it. Another began going to live concerts at least once a month, something that lit him up but which he'd never thought to do because he didn't have anyone in his life who shared his taste in music.

In the world of relationships, I constantly hear men and women talk about how their better halves have changed over the years and how unsatisfied they've become with their partners. Why? Some people will chalk it up to a change in interest level and tell you the new shine has worn off, and while that does happen, it only goes to show why I encourage prospective couples to choose each other for both shine and substance. And why I encourage them to maintain self-love and self-care practices before, during, and after their relationships. Breakups happen and the only relationship that is truly "'til death do us part" is the one we have with ourselves.

If you find a prospective partner with a quality character who has done enough soul-searching to be capable of being by themselves, and if you, in turn, have learned how to be comfortable inside your skin, your relationship will have what is required to go the distance. You will be able to communicate with confidence and mutual respect and not be looking to one another to spackle all the empty places inside yourself.

The process of becoming ready to date doesn't require you to be perfect to put yourself out there to meet someone else and it's not even something you can cross off the proverbial To-Do list. We should all be evolving in our relationships with others and with ourselves. Read books that challenge you to develop yourself, listen to podcasts, engage in spiritual exercises, see a therapist, consult a life coach, pursue your passions, take yourself on dates and anything else that makes you feel good about who you are, and you'll be coming to dating will a full life rather than an empty one.

I'm a huge believer that, when out on a date, you want to be looking to see if the person you're with likes themselves and enjoys their own company. If they don't, the likelihood of them being comfortable growing together with a partner is slim, and within a few months or years, you'll have grown apart.

The first time my heart had been broken, the beast inside that I had tried to suppress was released. In a matter of an hour, I lost my childhood best friend from birth and the love of my life from six grade until twenty-one in one fell swoop. Without going into detail, it would be easy to say that, when you put people together long enough while you are off pursuing your dream, things happen. I'm not sure, on my end, if these things would have happened, but they did and I moved on, but not without learning some things about myself. If this hadn't happened, I probably would have never discovered this about myself or men in general.

For almost five years after this break-up, with both friends and romantic relationships, I would not allow myself to become close to anyone. Like going through emotional rehab, I swore off allowing friendships to develop, and I didn't allow myself to open my heart to another woman.

I won't say I was a player because I believe not all men are players. And while I know many women would argue that point, if any man was like me when they entered their first relationship—committed to the end to be a great guy—only to discover your other half did not share the same level of commitment to your heart, he, too, would be reserved in future relationships.

I know, for women, it is difficult to separate the good men from the bad ones, especially if you are the kind of person who chooses to believe what is said to you until the speaker proves that you can't believe anything they say.

The person you are out on a date with can tell you anything. In most cases when we are dating, we set up things by giving up so much information that the person at the start becomes the person you tell them you are looking for. That works until they become too exhausted of being what you want and start to reveal who they really are. See, *words* are easy and require little to no effort and are easy to cover up, but *actions* are a tough act to follow and even tougher to fake. This is the reason, for almost five years after my childhood sweetheart broke up with me, that my heart and mind were closed off to developing a friendship with a male I could trust or a relationship with a female to whom I could trust my hear., I became *that guy*. Not full time, but I was *that guy*—the guy I'd said I would never be. I became that guy who wanted to be with a woman, but never said, "I love you" or "I've wanted to be with you forever." For years, I fought off who I was and fought off the guy I was becoming and never really wanted to be.

I invested very little time in developing either friendships or relationships. Every personal relationship was superficial, meaning the emotional return on investment was only on the surface, never allowing myself to let a feeling run too deep. Now, please, before you think about burning this book, make a note, I did not become *that guy* who got women's attention just for sex. I was far from *that* guy. I was still hurting, emotionally shut down, and did not allow anyone to get close enough to my heart to hurt me again. I put as little into developing a relationship as I could back then, just enough time to have a superficial phone conversation, and to take a woman out on a date. I never wanted to be asked in or to stay over, wanting, instead, to be alone, but not actually being alone. My actions did not support what was in my heart, and I had to shut down Kevin and reintroduce to the Kevin-I-was-then to the Kevin-I-wanted-to-be-going-forward. Exposing this emotional time of my life is not something I am proud of, but I am not the man today that I was yesterday.

It is your everyday actions that will determine the investment in you and in your relationship(s). The conversations I've had—and continue to have—with you throughout this book will cover the heart of both men and women partners and yes, those progressive women who now dominate a space once proudly held by their male counterparts.

Just to be fair and avoid the trolls, depending on your personal choice of partner and how you connect emotionally or psychologically at this moment, someone that is now all in will invest the absolute minimum amount of time to get your attention and affection to get what they desire most right now. They will cook a home-cooked meal for you, take you a picnic and wine in the park, tell you they love you, take you to the most expensive restaurant in town, look into your eyes and tell you that you are more special than anyone else they have ever met. But that will only last from Friday to Saturday night, and then Sunday and Monday come. They are too busy with work but will send you a one- or two-word text just to keep you on the hook. A game, maybe or maybe not, but it is something to think about. They may be playing the game of chance with your heart. We live in an instant society, and because of the lack of patience, we tend to put an exclamation on everything, including matters of the heart. Which leaves us open to think maybe it's too good to be true, or he or she is just like the last one, I moved to fast, because they leave us sitting on the side of the bed the next morning, wondering if they will want to see us again.

It took me five years to get over myself, which is the reason I believe we need to take time to date ourselves after a breakup or some other emotional loss. Now, when I say I love someone, my actions support that statement. A person is either into you or they are not. If you notice inconsistencies in how a person treated you when you first met compared to how they are treating you right now, and your gut is telling you that this isn't a good fit for you, do something about it. If the relationship takes more from you than it adds, then trust your gut. As I have told my daughters and the daughters of people that I have had this kind of conversations with (this holds for men, too) the amount of effort someone puts into dating you and trying to be with you beyond just sex will determine the return on your emotional investment.

As much as I would like to say I want to be the best guy and not like all the others, I don't believe there is such a thing as a perfect guy. Nor do I believe there is a perfect woman. Neither exists. But some out there have put the time in on working on themselves, and their actions synchronize with their words—that's a good thing.

Before you can add someone to your life, you must be true to the life you are living and understand how to love, date, and connect with yourself. We are all damaged by one thing or another, but we are all trying to be good people. However, everything must start and end with you.

Love starts from the inside. Truth pays for space in the same place where the lies live, and what your date will witness and remember goes far beyond your words but will hold you to the truth behind your actions.

It's not what you say to a person that they will remember, it's what you *do* to them that they will never forget. We are judged on our actions, not so much on our words, but the two, at times are inseparable.

Here's a truth that has nothing to do with dating, and more of what I learn about human behavior during 2021 and the world with Covid.

The truth is The Three "D's." As much as I would like to say this was a Kevin McLemore original, I got this from a conversation with a good friend, record producer Aaron Eubanks.

"Disagreements," "Disappointments," and "Dumb Shyt." Sound a lot like your last relationship?

CHAPTER TWENTY-FIVE

Permission To Touch, Be Touched, Kiss Or Be Kissed

Let's assume that your date is going great. The person you're sitting across from gives you that warm and fuzzy feeling. You look at them and it's as if the wind is blowing their hair and there's a soundtrack underscoring their every word and action. We've all been there. And if you haven't, hopefully, this book will help you create an atmosphere of romance that will have you there before you know it.

Maybe you and your date will be walking together on a beach or through a park. You could be seated in a restaurant or side-by-side at a show. Whatever you're doing and wherever you are, it's likely that, somewhere within the first few dates, there will be an opportunity for physical intimacy.

I've learned that romance isn't always something that arises on its own. Sexual inspiration is often a result of intentional action. Anyone who has ever been caught on the way to someone else's bedroom when they realize they forgot to buy contraceptives or who's feeling frisky but came over straight after work and didn't have time to take a shower will tell you that, when it comes to sex, failing to plan can result in failure to launch.

There are certain times when being unprepared can be trivial or inconsequential and others when it can be devastating.

When it comes to any form of physical intimacy, the two most important words you'll ever hear are *communication* and *consent*. I know that it can be scary to talk about sex. No one wants to face the possibility of rejection and it can be challenging to try to make it clear that your intentions are honorable while, at the same time, conveying significant interest. That said, if you can't talk about sex, you shouldn't be having it.

125

Chivalry doesn't need to be a lost art, but men should know that *assuming* isn't chivalrous; it's presumptuous. And invasive.

If you're a man out on a date, ask the one you're with, "Are you cold? Can I offer you, my jacket? Is it okay to kiss you? I'd love to take your hand..." Women should practice this, too. Despite what you may have been told, men aren't necessarily only after one thing and the more you treat a man like you value and respect him, the easier it will be for the two of you to be open with each other.

People might tell you that asking for permission strips the romance out of a situation, but that is far from the case. Communication is the sexiest thing there is. And if you can communicate well before you ever make it to the bedroom, when and if you do, the sex will be far better than anything you've ever known.

You've probably heard the old stereotype that men never ask for directions. Well, I'm here to tell you that, when it comes to dating, asking for and accepting directions is one of the most important things you can do.

Self-professed "players" will tell you they're like master chefs. They know the right ingredients, set the right temperature, and serve a dish that will leave you more than satiated. But whether at a restaurant or on a date, most people enjoy looking at the menu and placing their own order. Sure, they'll know what they're getting in advance, but the expectation is almost as delicious as its satisfaction.

Let yourself ask for what you want and need or, at the very least, voice what you are and are not open to.

Every date is a new experience, and every person is their own individual with wants, needs, and desires. Very few of us can read someone else's thoughts so, rather than attempting to take the simple step of asking to put your jacket over your date's shoulder or suggesting how nice it would be to be kissed.

If you're especially brave, I would suggest communicating your expectations around intimacy. For one person, a kiss is just a kiss, whereas, for another, it might suggest the start of a relationship. I know people for whom sex is a sacred act between soulmates and others who see it as nothing more than a fun act of friction. You don't need to have explicitly sexual conversations on a first date (in fact, I'd advise against that), but it's important to get a sense of someone else's views of intimacy before embarking on a path that might leave you heartbroken in the end.

Personally, I don't put myself out there to be rejected. In my business life, my confidence is over the top, but the dating me isn't as confident when comes to the signs that say it's okay to touch, be it holding hands or a kiss at the door. For whatever reason, I don't pick up the signs the way other guys do. However, growing up with a southern upbringing, I need to see the rockets' red glare before I will go out of my way to move in for a kiss or a hand-to-hand walk through the park.

Not all guys are dogs. Some of us still respect a woman and are willing to wait until we both agree to take the next step. But dating has become more progressive, and women are a lot more outgoing and more open to conversations about what they need and want. That can be good or bad, depending on the two people involved.

I once set two good friends up on a date, and, at the end of the evening, everything was perfect. After he walked her to her door and they exchanged pleasantries, he hopped back into the limo and left. When she called me to tell me about the date, she said everything was perfect, but she complained, to my surprise, that he didn't try anything. No touching, no handholding, and he never attempted to go in for a good night kiss. Nor did he wait long enough for her to invite him up to her place to continue their earlier conversation. She hadn't wanted the evening to end, but he was so nice, so perfect, that she said that she could not see him again because he was *too* nice, and she was afraid she'd hurt him.

I guess he was a lot like me—unless the signs are as clear as a bat signal projecting high in the clouds, some of us can miss the signs from our dates on each side. So, my suggestion would be to revert to the cards to help facilitate conversation about permission to have this evening end with more than just a good night out on the town.

CHAPTER TWENTY-SIX
Make Successful Mistakes

I have met couples who have overcome infidelity, financial hardships, difficult in-laws, health diagnoses, the loss of loved ones (including their children), and still somehow managed to emerge even more in love than ever.

After talking to some of these couples, I have come to realize that the biggest determinant of whether a relationship will succeed or not is not external factors or one partner's mistakes or lapses in judgment. The thing that keeps successful couples thriving is their ability to grow *together* rather than apart.

In a dating context, looking for someone who has the capacity to forgive and grow is important. You also want to cultivate these abilities within yourself. That doesn't mean you shouldn't have deal-breakers and high standards—you absolutely should. For me, for example, infidelity, lack of trust, and support are deal-breakers. For someone else, financial mismanagement or a descent into addiction might be. We all have the things we can cope with, and this isn't right or wrong. But struggles are an inevitable part of growing as a couple and you want to be on the lookout for someone with the maturity to move through them strongly and with a sense of connection.

When you realize a person's shortcomings, look to see how vested they are in learning from their mistakes and if they are looking to improve. It can be tempting to want someone willing to change for you, but don't let yourself fall for this seductive, but ultimately destructive, trap. You want to find a partner who is committed to self-improvement for *themselves*, as opposed to for you or the relationship. People who try to change for someone else are likely to alter their behavior for precisely as long as it takes to win another person's approval and then revert back to their previous ways. This can cause all sorts of inevitable backlash. For example, I had a client who told me about having lost fifty pounds in search of love only to gain it all back immediately following the walk to the altar. Is it any wonder their new spouse felt deceived when their fitness junkie quickly turned into a McDonald's devotee? A friend of mine told me about meeting his girlfriend at church, only to later discover she'd gone there solely to meet a man. She considered herself more of an agnostic. It's not that there's anything wrong with a lapse in faith or a diversion from a diet, but these examples speak to people who embarked on a certain path with the sole intention of getting a mate. Once they reached that goal, they had no more need to "pretend." The behavior itself wasn't the issue, the pretending was. If you learn nothing else from this book, I hope you learn that pretending has no place in dating.

One of the sincerest statements I heard a man say to his new girlfriend was, "I entered this relationship sideways, so I understand if you don't trust me. I'm damaged and I am working to be and do better for myself first and then for you."

The man who said this was a dear friend of mine who met a new potential partner before the ink on his divorce decree was dry. Time has yet to reveal if this new relationship will last, but the couple seems to be happy, and they were recently engaged. I credit my friend's sincere admission of his faults and failings and his commitment to hold himself accountable.

Even the best relationships have problems. They may have more problems than their dysfunctional counterparts because partners who are committed to growing together and moving forward have the sort of open and honest communication that acknowledges issues rather than seeks to avoid them.

From your very first date, you want to invest your time in learning about the other person and especially in learning how they deal with challenges and circumstances. You can learn a lot from a potential partner by looking at how they deal with not getting their way, how they pick themselves up after a fall, their willingness to take responsibility for their struggles, and the way they fight. Yes—every couple who lasts and has healthy communication and a loving connection has learned to fight constructively.

There's a quote I love, that isn't necessarily *about* relationships, but

I think it does apply to them. Denzel Washington said, "Nothing in life is worthwhile unless you take risks. Fall forward."

Dating is all about falling forward. It's about making mistakes, learning, and growing, arguing, and evolving. In a healthy relationship, you can disagree while still respecting and loving each other. You can learn from mistakes, amend your behavior, and fall forward. It's no accident that Denzel and his wife have been together since 1977.

There is no true science to what makes relationships work. There's no fifty-fifty split, no scorecard, no exact formula, but there are several qualities you can cultivate that will go a long way to ensuring success. Compromise, teamwork, positivity, kindness, generosity, authenticity, and mutual respect go a long way toward creating a relationship worth having.

When you learn positive ways of expressing your feelings, you reduce the chance of conflict and provide wonderful experiences, allowing other positive opportunities to blossom, without those emotional obstructions that created emotional roadblocks.

When you share your life with others, you learn that the act of giving of yourself is much more fun than the act of getting.

When the old ways aren't working, release yourself from those tired patterns.

When you are true to yourself and vested in making your partnership work, you can experience happiness both within yourself and with another person.

Success in dating isn't about what you do, it's not about who or what you were or are, it is simply when you have reached a point where you can make a successful mistake that will move your dating life forward.

CHAPTER TWENTY-SEVEN
The Five T's And One F

There are five T's that, when combined, will create a good relationship: time, talk/listen, touch, tenderness, and touch. Oh, add Forgiveness

1. **Time.**

   One of the major complaints in most relationships is time. Making time for your date, your kids, your pets, your parents, and your work can be a massive juggling act. For my female readers, please don't throw stones at me, but every man will tell you that women love to talk, and at the start of any friendship or relationship, both sexes spend a lot of time talking. Early on, that man sitting across from you hears every word you're saying. But if asked to repeat the last few things you said, he'll struggle to repeat it. Why? Because the mind of a man works better when you speak succinctly.

   Before you use this book to fuel the fire to boil the water you plan to throw me into, pause for a second to know that making quality time is essential in relationships and that you deserve to be heard, but it will help the relationship if you learn to share in ways that work for both of you. So, let a man know what matters and what you need from him, but also know that, just because he does not communicate the way you do, does not mean he isn't paying attention.

2. **Talk and listen.**

   Most secure men and women are looking for a partner who is not afraid to express their opinions or disagree. No one wants to be with a *yes-man* or *-woman*. When you are asked out on a first date, the universal question is, "What do you like to do?" This question is not open-ended. It is very direct. If you like going to the gym, then *say* you like going to the gym. If you like bike riding, reading, going to plays, walking the dog, et cetera, all these reveal to your date that you have a life. Your responses will show you have passions and reveal just how much you can contribute.

Understand that this is the first date for both of you. Don't start complaining about everything that has gone wrong in your life. Your date has their own problems. If you come across as needy people, it won't serve either of you.

No one wants to be with someone who is always complaining about something or someone because then you're not contributing anything to the friendship or relationship. Talk means to *talk*, not to *complain*. Complaining puts a burden on the relationship. You become too dependent, and you become disposable.

3. Touch (non-sexual)

When a woman says she enjoys being touched, a man's thoughts tend to turn to sex. If she says she wants to try new things, his thoughts are likely to veer toward sex. As I have mentioned before, men are simple, and women tend to be more complicated. The man sitting across from you right now needs to feel connected, and his ways of achieving that might differ from yours.

Physical touch for a woman is less likely to be sexual on some days than others depending on her needs and wants. Both sexes share the need to be desired and crave positive feedback, love, and tender touch. The stereotype is that men want sex more than women, but a lot of people hunger for physical touch, and this should be a healthy and mutually enjoyable part of a relationship.

Most of the men I interviewed for this book expressed wanting the women in their lives to initiate touch and sex and connection. There are so many books out there telling women how to get a man and keep him interested that advise playing "hard to get," but this makes women suppress their very natural desire and makes men feel as if they're constantly being rejected. So initiate touch when you want it, and don't do it if you don't want to.

4. Tenderness

When a relationship falls apart or there are issues with the foundation of your relationship and you peel back the layers, you will discover that the things that brought you together are no longer happening. Back in the day when the two of you first met, you both went out of your way to do what the other liked. If she liked going to plays, you both went to plays. If he followed a football team and she followed another, you took turns watching each team, but you both cheered for each other's team if the other's weren't in the championship playoffs. What brought the two of you together and kept the two of you interested was likely being tender and kind to each other.

5. **Trust.**

The biggest pitfall in any relationship or friendship is losing trust. Because of past experiences, we are all emotionally broken. What someone else has done to you in the past should not be the topic of conversation with the person you are sitting across from right now. The sole purpose of *Dating With A Full Deck* is to create open and honest dialogue. You are not with this person now to be deceptive and emotionally manipulative. Both of you want to be assured that the other can be trusted, and you want to believe in their character. Keep this in mind and do not deviate from this in the slightest *unless* either of you gives the other a reason to lose that trust. I do not believe in love at first sight. I interviewed a couple who did, and they are living happily-ever-after. Therefore, there *is* the possibility that there is an undeniable spark that can connect two to become one. Trust is big. Most of the time when you are not able to give trust, it gives an underlying notion that you cannot be trusted. Therefore, you are on autopilot when it comes to trusting others. Honesty starts with you. You must know who you are and know you can be trusted. We have all played those games with the wrong person, but, right now, we are starting with a clean slate. What is behind us is just that, behind us. *Until* given a reason not to trust your date.

6. **Forgiveness**

Involves a deep sense of understanding yourself, your insecurities, your guard over your heart, your common sens/gut, and stepping out from your place of safety. In the right relationship and with the right person, depending on the issues or problem, by replacing the *why* and, for the moment, stand in your partner's shoes, sometimes you discover grace. What may be a dealbreaker from some, may be dealmaker if both you and your partner can learn from whatever mistake either partner is facing right now. Forgiveness comes from a strong place in your heart. Faith is a superpower. If your partner exercises this superpower, and you are the benefactor, consider yourself blessed and protect this gift. You only get one to two chances at real love, everything after that is just another date or relationship.

CHAPTER TWENTY-EIGHT

Real Players Win

I have been pondering a way to end this book without becoming too redundant or didactic. One of the things I want to leave you with is how to use the cards in the book on your first date and explain the 53rd and 54th card in the deck—The Jokers.

The Joker has no face value, nor does it have a conversation associated with it. Depending on what emotional game you're playing within yourself, these two cards can be the most powerful in the deck because they allow the person who draws them to circle back to one of the conversation cards the other opted not to talk about, did not elaborate on, or left some question unanswered, which now has to be addressed. Note, remember the date is supposed to be fun, so don't browbeat your date over a conversation they opt not to have. These cards allow you to open up a little more, dive deeper into what you think you heard or have may left out, or maybe have shifted in your position because of present company.

So why should *Dating With A Full Deck* be any different?

Because both parties agreed to follow the rule, long before the first date. Each person must read the book before the first date starts. The person that invited you out for the date must bring all 54 cards to the date with them.

The first date is all about fun, so the only conversation to be had must follow the flip and reading the content on the card.

Please keep this simple, there are 54 playing cards that come with each book, 52 have a content question that allows both of you to ask a ques-tion and allow your date to give their response, creating open and honest conversation between two people. If all goes well, those 54 cards should create an hour and a half of truthful conversation.

137

You also must remember that the premise of *Dating With A Full Deck* is not how to get a man or woman, but there is a possibility that, when two people meet, have common interests, and, at some point, may get into a relationship. "The risk and the reward."

You must understand that you have been dealing with another human being and that you have a responsibility to be as kind and as respectful to your date as you would require them to be to you. I'm not a firm believer in hooking up on the very first date or in love at first sight.

However, I have learned that love is possible if your heart is in it and you're true to yourself. A quick hook-up can be good if the two people are in the same emotional state and can live with the decision of the night before or the morning after.

So, with that said, no book can truly outline a list of rules of *Do*'s and *Don't*s that will guarantee you a happy ending. Having a clear understanding of human behavior, of who you are are, provide the only truths in any relationship.

No one on this planet will be able to produce a document or statistic to cover every situation when it comes to emotions and affairs of the heart or what you could do that will cover all the bases for anyone to master the art of dating. But there *is* this book which will act as your wingman when you are out on the first date. It can give you a certain level of confidence, so you'll lessen the chances of screwing up the first date with someone you are truly interested in and setting up the possibility of Date Number Two.

So, without saying much more, I will end the book with this: men, women, and partners set dating traps for each other, which is the reason many have been in failed relationships. Both men and women must weed out the bad ones and decide to not settle for less than either deserves.

I do hope that this book and the accompanying deck of playing cards create open and honest conversation. I hope you apply the relationship conversations I've shared with you in both your dating life and the rest of your life.

So, "live your life, like it was the last day on earth." "Laugh like it was how you made your living, and love like you were writing your own story. It would be up to you as to the ending, drama, comedy, adventure, horror, or the best love story ever told.

Thank you.

Kevin McLemore. (The modern-day Hitch)

DATING WITH A FULL DECK

PLAYING CARDS (52 CARDS, PLUS TWO JOKERS)

DATING
with a   FULL
DECK

DATING
with a   FULL
DECK

A

If your date had food in their teeth, would you tell them? If yes, tell me what you say.

2

If your pet and your lover both fell into the water and were drowning and you could only save one, which would you save?

3

If your lover's best friend is cheating on their partner and you find out, would you tell the partner? Why or why not?

4

If you were playing strip poker in the outfit you're wearing right now, what article of clothing would you give up first?

DATING
with a FULL
DECK

DATING
with a FULL
DECK

DATING
with a FULL
DECK

DATING
with a FULL
DECK

5 ♦

If you had one thing that you could say to your date, knowing you would never see him/her again, what would you say?

6 ♦

What is more important to you, a person's past, or their future?

7 ♦

Trust is a piece of glass. Once it's been broken, it can never be perfect again. What's a time you broke someone's trust, or they broke yours? Were you a fixer or a destroyer? What happened to the glass? ♦

8 ♦

If you were stranded on a deserted island, with all your basic physical needs met but no chance of being rescued, what six things would you take with you to occupy your time? ♦

DATING *with a* **FULL** **DECK**

DATING *with a* **FULL** **DECK**

DATING *with a* **FULL** **DECK**

DATING *with a* **FULL** **DECK**

9 ◆

What is the number one quality you look for in a friend and/or a partner?

◆
6

10 ◆

What are three things you would like to know about your date? Tell your date the three things you would like your date to know about you.

◆
01

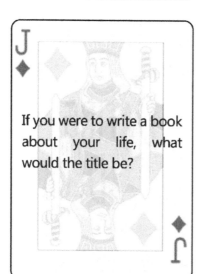

J ◆

If you were to write a book about your life, what would the title be?

◆
ſ

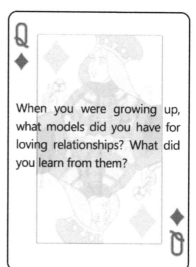

Q ◆

When you were growing up, what models did you have for loving relationships? What did you learn from them?

◆
Ø

DATING *with a* **FULL DECK**

DATING *with a* **FULL DECK**

DATING *with a* **FULL DECK**

DATING *with a* **FULL DECK**

A ♣

When things don't go the way you want, how do you handle disappointment?

 ♣ **A**

 2 ♣

How do you take care of yourself physically, emotionally, mentally, and spiritually?

 ♣ **2**

 3 ♣

What are the top five things on your bucket list?

 ♣ **3**

4 ♣

What are the top three qualities you look for in a partner?

 ♣ **4**

DATING
with a FULL
DECK

DATING
with a FULL
DECK

DATING
with a FULL
DECK

DATING
with a FULL
DECK

5
♣

If my parents or friends didn't like you, how would that make you feel about me if I said nothing and what would you do or say to me? Would it affect our relationship?

 5

6
♣

What are your biggest pet peeves?

9

7
♣

How do you prefer to spend your weekends?

L

8
♣

What makes you emotionally, physically happy, spiritually happy, and happy on an intellectual level?

♣
8

DATING
with a **FULL**
DECK

DATING
with a **FULL**
DECK

DATING
with a **FULL**
DECK

DATING
with a **FULL**
DECK

9♣

Do you still live with your parents and if yes, tell me why?

9♣

10♣

Tell me about your first kiss.

10♣

J♣

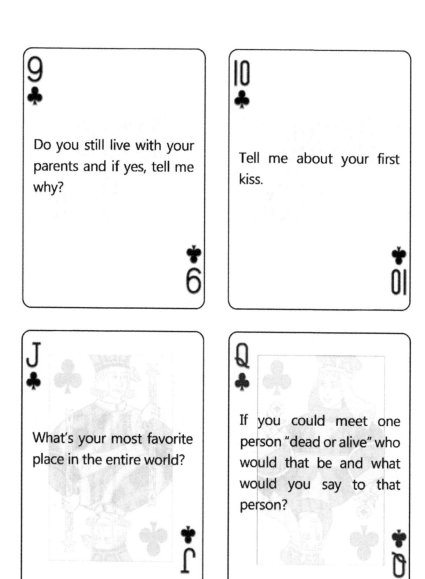

What's your most favorite place in the entire world?

J♣

Q♣

If you could meet one person "dead or alive" who would that be and what would you say to that person?

Q♣

DATING
with a FULL
DECK

DATING
with a FULL
DECK

DATING
with a FULL
DECK

DATING
with a FULL
DECK

If you could meet the 16-year-old you know, what would you say to the younger you about how you have lived your life?

What's your biggest goal in life right now?

3
♥

What is your go-to distraction when you need a break?

4
♥

What activity is guaranteed to keep you focused and engaged?

DATING
with a FULL
DECK

DATING
with a FULL
DECK

DATING
with a FULL
DECK

DATING
with a FULL
DECK

5 ♥ What turns you on more? A) A home cooked meal by candlelight, prepared by you B) Dinner and wild night in the town. C) Warm bubble bath, chocolate covered strawberries and white wine and a foot massage. D) A cozy sleep over on the beach?

6 ♥ How much does winning matter to you?

7 ♥ Do you respect your partner's personal items? If yes or no, explain why.

8 ♥ How do you resolve problems, or do you hold grudges?

DATING
with a FULL
DECK

DATING
with a FULL
DECK

DATING
with a FULL
DECK

DATING
with a FULL
DECK

9
♠

Have I said or done anything on this date that has turned you off?

♥
6

10
♠

How would you like this date to end? With a hug, long walk, holding hands and a small kiss or wishing you would have stayed home with a glass of wine and ice cream?

♥
01

J
♠

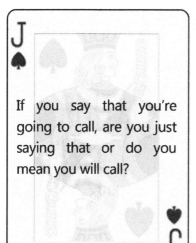

If you say that you're going to call, are you just saying that or do you mean you will call?

♥
ſ

Q
♠

What's the most romantic thing you've ever experienced?

♥
Ὁ

DATING with a **FULL DECK**

DATING with a **FULL DECK**

DATING with a **FULL DECK**

DATING with a **FULL DECK**

A ♠

What are your favorite quotes and why?

♥ A ♠

 2 ♠

What are your feelings on pets and your relationship?

♥ 2 ♠

 3 ♠

Tell me about your future and what you want most out of life?

♥ 3 ♠

 4 ♠

Can you be trusted with my heart?

♥ 4 ♠

DATING
with a FULL
DECK

DATING
with a FULL
DECK

DATING
with a FULL
DECK

DATING
with a FULL
DECK

5 ♠

Which would you rather be: four hundred pounds or $400,000 in debt?

5

6 ♠

Do you have a sense of passion and purpose? What lights you up and inspires you?

9

7 ♠

What are the ways in which you have changed and evolved over time?

7

8 ♠

What advice did you get before this date, and who gave it to you?

8

DATING *with a* FULL DECK

DATING *with a* FULL DECK

DATING *with a* FULL DECK

DATING *with a* FULL DECK

9 ♠

Have I said or done anything on this date that has turned you off?

♥ 6

10 ♠

How would you like this date to end? With a hug, long walk, holding hands and a small kiss or wishing you would have stayed home with a glass of wine and ice cream?

♥ 01

J ♠

If you say that you're going to call, are you just saying that or do you mean you will call?

♥ ſ

Q ♠

What's the most romantic thing you've ever experienced?

♥ Ø

DATING
with a FULL
DECK

DATING
with a FULL
DECK

DATING
with a FULL
DECK

DATING
with a FULL
DECK

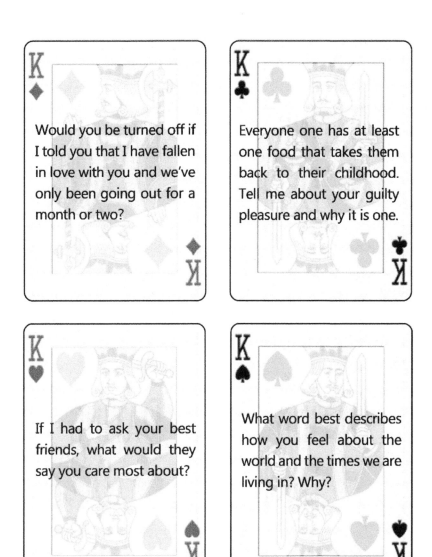

K ♦

Would you be turned off if I told you that I have fallen in love with you and we've only been going out for a month or two?

K ♣

Everyone one has at least one food that takes them back to their childhood. Tell me about your guilty pleasure and why it is one.

K ♥

If I had to ask your best friends, what would they say you care most about?

K ♠

What word best describes how you feel about the world and the times we are living in? Why?

DATING
with a **FULL**
DECK

DATING
with a **FULL**
DECK

DATING
with a **FULL**
DECK

DATING
with a **FULL**
DECK

About the Author

P. Kevin McLemore is a humble man of great passion and zest for life, who has devoted a lifetime to motivating people and pursuing and achieving everything he has set out to accomplish. Being raised by his grandparents, he learned the most important traits about human emotions, about being kind, having character, setting big goals, and chasing down your dreams like you stole them and were getting away.

His father always said that, out of all his kids, Kevin would run to the edge of a cliff and while all his sister brothers were looking over the edge to see how far it was to fall, Kevin would just jump, knowing he would always land on his feet. Dad was right; that's Kevin to a T. He believes in trying something new and that anything is possible, which is why his career and personal life reflect this positive, risk-taking attitude.

Kevin has never wavered in his resolution to set audacious goals and, not always but most of the time, has been successful. He has professionally gained the reputation of being one of the best fitness professionals and lifestyle coaches in the business, which is the reason he took on a project such as this one.

Kevin is President of RMK Production and the 10 United Podcast network, Co-host "Talking "wit" Kevin and son" the podcast, he also has made amazing accomplishments as a strength and endurance coach, track and field coach, athlete, marketing specialist, QVC pitchman, and master level fitness professional, coached IRONMAN athletes as well as three squash world champions. He has a lifelong passion to work with various youth groups and be a television spokesperson. Kevin became a first-time author with the *Letters to Elvis*. He has recently finished his third book *The Indispensable Game Of X's and O's; How I Learned Everything I'd Ever Needed To Know About Life By Playing High School Football.* Upcoming books are *57 And I Can,* and *The Truth About Health and*

KEVIN MCLEMORE

Fitness, and more. He intends to produce an animated Christmas story from his award-winning book, "Distinguished Authors Guild Award" Sprinkles, *The True Spirit Of Christmas*, which is another extension of how he wants to continue to help improve other people's lives.

Made in the USA
Middletown, DE
01 September 2022

72118294R00106